UNF*CK

YOUR LIFE AND RELATIONSHIPS

UNF*CK

YOUR LIFE AND RELATIONSHIPS

How lessons from
my life can help you
build healthy
relationships from
the inside out

Anita Astley

M.ED., LMFT, Psychotherapist

Forefront
BOOKS

Published by Forefront Books.
Distributed by Simon & Schuster.

Library of Congress Control Number: 2022910864

Print ISBN: 978-1-63763-123-2
E-book ISBN: 978-1-63763-124-9

Cover Design by Bruce Gore, GORE STUDIO, INC.
Interior Design by Mary Susan Oleson, BLU DESIGN CONCEPTS

I DEDICATE THIS BOOK to my mother, Vimlesh Peetush, and my father, Tulsi Ram Peetush, who both taught me the value of a strong work ethic and worked hard to afford me opportunities that were beyond their reach. For that I am eternally grateful.

More specifically, I would like to thank my mother for her unconditional love and support. She was always there to lift me up when I was down and served as my security blanket when I most needed shelter from the world. She modeled peace in her very being and taught me to find peace within myself and my circumstances. She is an amazingly strong woman. My strength is a testimony to hers.

And to my father, I am ironically grateful for some of our years of sparring, although at the time I never thought I would ever feel this way. Those experiences helped cultivate my resilience and nurtured my ability to fight and survive in the world. And in the later years when I was able to meet my father for the first time as a man rather than as my father, I learned that in his prime he was a man of action, perseverance, determination, vision, and great passion. I am my father's daughter.

TABLE *of* CONTENTS

FOREWORD.. 9

PREFACE.. 13

INTRODUCTION.. 15

PART 1: Building Healthy Relationships from the Inside Out

1: UNF*CK Awareness: Self-Awareness and Self-Care.......................................25

2: UNF*CK Thoughts & Emotions: Projection and Passive-Aggressive Behavior..... 83

PART 2: Working Together

3: UNF*CK Talking: Verbal Communication 125

4: UNF*CK Mind Reading: Needs and Expectations 161

5: UNF*CK Blurred Lines: Boundaries... 209

6: UNF*CK Conflict: Stop Avoiding and Start Confronting 229

7: UNF*CK Happiness: Forgiveness, Acceptance, and Contentment 257

SUMMARY 275

ACKNOWLEDGMENTS 283

NOTES 287

FOREWORD

AUTHOR TOM ROBBINS has famously and memorably said, " . . . we, each of us, are responsible for our own fulfillment. Nobody else can provide it for us, and to believe otherwise is to delude ourselves dangerously and to program for eventual failure every relationship we enter."[1]

Anita Astley's career as a student at McGill University was nothing short of a brilliant journey toward self-actualization of that maxim that would make Maslow, the father of needs-fulfillment theory, proud. This is why I passionately believe and can certify that when Anita Astley arrived at McGill, which is top-ranked worldwide among universities, where she sought out the opportunities associated with higher education, she was one of those rare students who already understood Robbins's wise remark. Perhaps it was her multicultural background, her personal challenges experienced and conquered as a young adult, her strong and ambitious constitution, her ultimate desire to leave her unique imprint on the world. In any case, as she entered the graduate program in the faculty of the Department of Educational & Counselling Psychology speaking French, Hindi, and English, she had a great thirst for knowledge and was dedicated to this fulfillment most positively.

I should know. I am a McGill professor emeritus and an author of many books, tests, journal articles, and educational programs published by Rutledge, Scholastic, Kendall-Hunt, Allyn & Bacon, and Lawrence Erlbaum Associates. My research has emphasized the qualitative study of classrooms as cultures and, especially, the use of qualitative methods to understand how to support inquiry-based learning at all levels of education. That makes me most qualified to endorse, authenticate, and even substantiate her credentials in the current mode of application, which makes her advice the more real and advantageous to all interested parties.

Initially, I met Anita when she enrolled in an introductory qualitative-research course offered to graduate students in the department, but already I could see greatness in her, vis-à-vis her fiery ambition. Along those lines of mentor and mentee, Carl Jung once said, "The meeting of two personalities is like the contact of two chemical substances: if there is any reaction, both are transformed."[2] This is how I'd like to think of my relationship with Anita, since I will forever be changed for the better by my knowing her and her inspiring story of surmounting obstacles by using their very fabric as fuel for her journey and the tutelage of getting there.

I have learned so much in how I was privileged to teach her, and yet, like all great professors who learn from their students, I also was educated if not enlightened by her; that is,

FOREWORD

by her generous spirit, her agile mind, and other gifted qualities that were evident from the very beginning. For example, it took very little time to learn that Anita was also a gifted listener and a keen observer of human interactions. She exhibited the natural curiosity and sensitivity needed to make the strange familiar. I still remember her case study of a street musician and her active participation in class discussions. She displayed an enthusiasm for learning, especially in regard to interpersonal dynamics that all professors wish of their students.

Because of this keen faculty and her natural gifts, I employed Anita in the summer of 1995 as a graduate assistant. She completed a qualitative graduate thesis under my direction. And, of course, her work, as always, was careful, analytic, and insightful. Consequently, I encouraged her to pursue a PhD, also under my direction, as I believed she would be an excellent candidate and student. However, Anita's heart and passion were in pursuing a career in psychotherapy, not in instruction, which was my focus of research. As all ideal mentors do of their mentees, I supported Anita in her desire to enter the helping and healing profession. Indeed, in consequence, I knew then as I do today that it was and is her calling in life. Over the years, we have remained in touch, and I have been a witness to her growth and metamorphosis not only as a woman but as a brilliant psychotherapist. I know she has helped many people transform their lives because she believes people can change despite circumstances. Her life is a testimony to "adversity building resilience." She is and ever will be, never the victim, always a survivor.

FOREWORD

Having seen her giving of herself, I heartily accept the motto that she confirms with her life's example and that motivational speaker Tony Robbins has expressed: "The only way a relationship will last is if you see your relationship as a place that you go to give, and not a place that you go to take."[3] Anita has always treated me this way, and I am sure this is how she relates to her clients. She is an amazingly supportive person who brings laughter, compassion, caring, and insightfulness to those she interacts with. She now has over twenty-five years of successful practice as a licensed individual, couples, and family psychotherapist, having been licensed in Quebec, New York, and now Wisconsin. I am most pleased to have the honor of recommending her new book to those of you reading this page. Using her knowledge, academic training, and excerpts from her own life story and those from her clients, she has created a book that nurtures and at the same time challenges us to reflect on our relationships, how they come to be, what they mean to us, and how through them we can become the best versions of ourselves.

—Mark W. Aulls, PhD

Professor Emeritus
Department of Educational
and Counselling Psychology,
McGill University

PREFACE

"UNF*CK YOUR LIFE AND RELATIONSHIPS" was not the original title for this book. The original title referenced benign elements such as metamorphosis and butterflies, suggested by one of my former editors. I accepted this advice, since my book is, admittedly, about the transformation of the self and relationships. More importantly, I thought this particular editor knew better about these matters and that this critical personal branding exercise was clearly outside of my lane. However, having sat for weeks with this other title, I became increasingly uncomfortable with the idea of portraying myself to you, dear reader, as something I am not. Butterflies are beautiful, of course, but they neither reflect who I am nor my voice. Most people who know me well would not make the association. The more I delved into the original manuscript, the more I concluded that the words told my story and shared my expert advice; however, the voice belonged to someone else; a difficult realization to arrive at while nearing completion of a project of this magnitude.

PREFACE

So I did what I always do in similar situations: I called a dear friend and explained my dilemma. During this conversation, I realized that I had unconsciously repeated something I had always done as a young woman: suppressed my voice, particularly as it related to my father, whom you will learn more about as you read my story. *How f*cked up is that?!* I thought to myself. Although I have *mostly* unf*cked all of that, I found myself unconsciously slipping into old patterns very quickly when triggered and not aware of my emotional vulnerabilities. Awareness is key, and actress and activist Sophia Bush is right: "You are allowed to be both a masterpiece and a work in progress, simultaneously." There is no shame in that!

As soon I became aware, I quickly unf*cked the situation, as unf*cking is what I do best. That conversation with my dear friend single-handedly led me to the title you see today: *Unf*ck Your Life and Relationships*. It's raw, it's real, and most important, it's me. Growing up with a father who often used profanity helped me become very comfortable with such language, although I recognize and appreciate that context is key. But in this context, "unf*cked" is the perfect term to describe my story and my process of becoming who I am today, personally and professionally. I had a pretty f*cked-up life, and equally f*cked-up relationships, until I learned how to unf*ck myself from the inside out. You can too.

INTRODUCTION

LET'S FACE IT: irrespective of who we are in the world, relationships inevitably f*ck us up. When our relationships are in turmoil, our lives are in turmoil. When our hearts hurt, our minds hurt; the two are intricately linked, and any attempt to deny the interplay between them is futile. The mind speaks to the heart, and the heart speaks to the mind, which leads to observable reactions stemming from feelings of sadness on one end of the emotional spectrum, to fulfillment on the other—with a lot of grey noise in between. I am certain you can relate to this as much as I can. This is a universal issue to which we bring our collective relational experiences: the good, the bad, and the ugly. Consequently, it is not a question of *if* we will experience turbulence in our relationships but a question of *when*.

When spending enough time sharing your thoughts and feelings with someone, you are rendering yourself vulnerable. Vulnerability is a pathway to building emotional intimacy, which, as expressed by many of my patients over the years, is something to be desired but also feared. Why? Emotional intimacy breeds

15

INTRODUCTION

conflict. The closer we get to someone, the more likely we will eventually experience some level of conflict, something most of us try to avoid. Although avoidance on the surface seems like an effective technique initially and is compatible with our desire to maximize pleasure and minimize pain, as so beautifully articulated by the founding father of "talk therapy," Sigmund Freud, in his 1920 essay "Beyond the Pleasure Principle," I assure you that it doesn't work and is short-lived. Most often, it leads to greater problems in the future as unresolved issues grow and metastasize over time and manifest as relational cancer. My personal challenges and professional experience as a licensed individual, couples, and family psychotherapist of over twenty-five years are a testament to this belief.

Unfortunately, to avoid the certainty of conflict and repeated negative relational experiences and getting f*cked up, many try to avoid relationships altogether and profess that they are not in any nor desire to be. Not possible. By nature, we are social animals, and it is in our DNA to pursue relationships. From our first breath, we are born into relationships with our parents, siblings, and extended family, and then with the world, once we are launched. These early experiences, for most, are conflicted, complex, and far from perfect; hence, our f*cked-upness.

Furthermore, relationships are truly unavoidable; we are all in one type of relationship or another, obviously with varying degrees of closeness: neighbors, friends, family members, coworkers, a significant other. And relationships today have also taken on different shapes and forms via social media and

INTRODUCTION

smartphones—unfortunately, escalating further relational challenges, especially regarding communication. These new unfamiliar heights are complicated and have created unnecessary entanglements, which I believe would not exist if not for the medium itself. E-communication is truly our best friend in one context and our worst enemy in another; it's a double-edged sword. Its addictive nature makes it virtually impossible to unplug ourselves when we need to and sometimes should, further adding to the complexities of life, love, our overall sense of connectedness, and our search for the perfect relationship that does not exist, except for an illusionary form of it on social media.

Let me be clear: perfection in relationships does not exist. The sooner you accept this notion, the easier and more fulfilling your relationships will be.

Consequently, when problems arise, as they inevitably do, you will not be surprised or disappointed but prepared to work through them and recognize that there are no shortcuts or quick fixes to unf*cking the mind, the heart, and your relationships. Relationships are the playgrounds for minds to unpack and dump your emotional and psychological baggage from childhood to adulthood. In the context of relationships, the past meets the present to resolve that which remains unresolved and displace unanchored thoughts, feelings, and behaviors. Consequently, the cycle of dysfunction repeats itself.

Perpetuate the cycle or break it? The choice is yours whether or not to unf*ck yourself and your relationships from the inside out.

INTRODUCTION

From the inside out? You will come across this phrase throughout the book; what does it mean? Most of us look for solutions and fault outside of ourselves; however, in attempting to unf*ck our relationships, we must begin with unf*cking the relationship we have with ourselves. And yes, we all have one! It's that internal voice that speaks to you, the one you sometimes have chosen to ignore, listen to, mute, or find a reason to argue. By the end of this book, you will be able to confront and embrace this inner voice, which will, in turn, help you unf*ck your life and then your relationships from the inside out. As a result, you will learn how to be the best version of yourself for your own individual growth and all those around you.

Clearly, you've picked up this book because you're looking for relief and change from your current f*cked-up situation. You're searching for something to permit you to do what you are too afraid to do or even admit to yourself. Denial is a powerful defense mechanism; it blurs our reflection in the mirror. I can sympathize. I know how the past frightens you, the thought of the future causes anxiety, and the present feels unsettling—perhaps even paralyzing. It's OK; I know your narrative well. I used to be you.

Today I am a strong, independent, confident, professional woman, comfortable in my dark skin. I have walked the walk and now I talk the talk as a clinician with more than a quarter-century of experience working with individuals, couples, and families. Yet I was the opposite for most of my childhood and young adult years. I would have been unrecognizable if you had met me thirty years ago. I was raised in a patriarchal Indian

INTRODUCTION

household where I was imprisoned by the hurtful and critical words of my father, who repeatedly reinforced the message that my "worth would be a function of my much-anticipated arranged marriage." I was told "how to be" and "who to be."

During my formative years, my identity was ascribed to me—particularly my cultural identity, which I could not accept nor wanted to accept. I was labeled a "stupid girl" because I struggled in school. Rather than receive help, I was mocked and called names. My father only saw the value of my education to barter for an educated husband, a cultural norm to which he subscribed. Although my mother tried to help, having grown up in a patriarchal culture and wed at sixteen, she did not have much power. Still, she was and has always been my saving grace.

Consequently, I had minimal self-worth for most of my young adulthood and rarely spoke. Sadly, I bought into the false narrative of my physical and intellectual inadequacies without any appreciation or mention of my beauty, an internal beauty I believe all children bring into the world and possess. My low self-worth kept dwindling until there was less and less of me and then none of me. Although I didn't realize it at the time, my cravings for love, validation, acceptance, and my search for value from a fatherly figure led me into an inappropriate relationship with an older man, a relationship I mistook for love but which years later, through my own individual therapy, realized had nothing to do with love but was a grave violation of my physical and emotional boundaries. I was only fifteen.

For a long time, I was a prisoner of my negative thoughts,

19

feelings, choices, and actions stemming from my family-of-origin dynamics. However, I learned to unf*ck myself and, in time, my relationships through much-needed individual therapy. I can help you do the same—show you how to free yourself from the limits you have ascribed and learn how to build healthy relationships from the inside out.

As a licensed clinician, I know the science and the theories. I have a master's from McGill University's Department of Educational and Counselling Psychology and post-graduate certification from the Argyle Institute of Human Relations in marriage and family therapy. But my science is about the science of what works. So this book is not an academic treatise but is geared toward real-world applications. It's comprehensive and practical and was written with your transformation in mind. You need help to change and improve your life and relationships. And I have laid out the pathway for you with the collective goal of building healthy relationships in your life.

My transformation and journey provide evidence, credibility, and some level of authority over the resistance and darkness of inter- and intrapersonal challenges. I am, by nature, experience, and profession, a solution-oriented person. That's my gift and my life's purpose. Time, a life lived, struggled with and conquered; adversity; and real-world experience have all honed my sense for and agency in solving people's relationship problems into an almost surgical sharpness and acumen that can serve you. My academic training and my personal story strengthened my ability to empathize with people's challenges in life and relationships. I see these challenges from a solution-oriented mindset. My goal always remains to help mobilize people from problems to solutions and, of course, to implement those solutions. The seven self-help strategies that make up this book are designed to equip you with the tools to do it yourself from the inside out.

The core message of this book is that you need to "get back to the basics" of building healthy relationships by mastering simple-yet-complicated dynamics. Simple because you are probably familiar with the language, but complicated in that they represent the layers of your history and, to a large degree, dictate how you interpret, analyze, and communicate your thoughts and feelings. These concepts are easy to state but challenging to apply. However, I am confident that you will be successful. This is because they are ultimately feasible, viable, achievable, attainable, actionable, and all-around doable.

In Part 1 of this book, I share aspects of my personal story with unflinching honesty. When I refer to painful memories, it is not to blame or shame my parents or others from my past but to inspire and motivate you to unf*ck yourself as I did. Adversity does truly build resilience!

People know what I do as a psychotherapist, but few know my why. Yet, it is this why that drives my passion for helping others get unf*cked from the inside out! My positive success rate with patients and the benefits of their results speak for themselves. Thus, I offer my own experience as proof of how life-changing, although basic, the methods I share and their applications to your life are. Life and relationships are messy and f*cked up—but they can be unf*cked.

INTRODUCTION

In Part 2 of the book, I provide specific prescriptions to help you unf*ck your life and relationships from the inside out. You will learn how to own your projections, set boundaries, resolve conflict, become a better listener, and other fundamental parts of building, nurturing, developing, and maintaining healthy relationships. Worksheets are provided at the end of each chapter to help you get started in applying what you have learned. I also encourage you to ask the significant others in your life to complete these worksheets to bring about a deeper understanding of the interpersonal dynamics in your relationships.

I am confident that by the end of this book, you will understand, appreciate, and internalize my two most revered mantras: "Our mental health hinges on the quality of our relationships" and "Building healthy relationships starts from the inside out." We *are* our relationships.

Let's begin . . .

PART 1

Building Healthy Relationships from the Inside Out

CHAPTER 1

UNF*CK AWARENESS:
Self-Awareness and Self-Care

I VIVIDLY REMEMBER the day I started to work from the inside out and began my journey of metamorphosis. I walked into my psychoanalyst's office feeling confident and strong. At least, that's what I wanted him to believe and had convinced myself of for years.

"I am only here for didactic purposes," I naively said. "It's a prerequisite for graduation, per my program." As if I had mastered the mystery of my life before I even knew what it was or started to address it. Thankfully, Dr. Frank knew better and had enough experience to see beyond my words.

Little did I know that this would be the most valuable

and unique relationship I could ever imagine with a gentleman twenty years my senior. Our therapeutic connection would not only later guide, shape, and inform my therapeutic approach, but it would help me heal and accept the wounded little girl within. I would learn how to live life on my terms and conditions, not hers. In hindsight, my time with Dr. Frank went far beyond meeting a prerequisite for my academic program to being a prerequisite for understanding how to build healthy relationships from the inside out.

CHANGE

Before I share more about my personal metamorphosis, I would like for you to think about the concept of change. Although most agree on its definition, there is much dispute among clinicians and theorists alike on how to help bring about change in people's lives. It's an interesting process to ponder, one that I have spent most of my career contemplating. Based on over twenty-five years of clinical experience and my personal challenges, I believe I have finally arrived at some concrete solutions that have constructive and heartening applications for all. In many ways, getting "back to the basics" of relating to one another has gotten lost as a result of our ever-evolving and conflicting relationships with various forms of electronic communication and social media. (I will address this in more detail in chapter 3.)

Embarking on the journey of change requires a degree of exploration of the past in an effort to understand the present and shape the future. As I say to my patients, "We need to visit the past, but we need not live there." Life is to be lived in the *here and now,* the present, with great hope, enthusiasm, and excitement. Yet the past, although gone, lives on through the theaters of our minds, via our thoughts, emotions, and actions. If we are to ultimately derive life-giving pleasure from our mental and relationship patterns, we must resolve as much as we can and learn not to engage in the negative patterns of seeking life from something, someone, or a time that no longer exists. The past cannot give life back to us, no matter how much we coax it with mental effort or delusional desire.

The words I uttered to my therapist thirty years ago, "I don't need to be here," I now often hear from my clients. This statement is usually followed by, "My spouse thinks I need to be here, but I'm fine." I understand the initial resistance to the process. Being encouraged to or deciding to seek therapy is a very difficult step, one that at first, by nature, is frightening.

However, therapy can be one of the most courageous, powerful, unique, and life-altering experiences. Looking back, I only wish my father had the privilege I had years ago. If he/ we had only done the work, little by little, the obstacle and the task of leveraging it by the process of introspection and self-awareness would have been simplified by time and effort, and, most important, by the love that I know was behind the dysfunction between us.

The dilemma and struggle to change is a function, or rather, the malfunction, of confusion and the dysfunction itself. This makes the mental, physical, and social status quos we have with ourselves and others doubly difficult, mired in the mental mud where our nature and self are meant to flower and even bloom toward life and love. That's why the so-called "shit" of our lives, which I often disturb with clients to get to the root of the problem, tends to make the best fertilizer for the plant and seeds of positive change.

This initial disinclination or even defiance toward the prospect of self-awareness, rooted in self-alienation, arises from a lack of clarity caused by being adrift in the dysfunction. One is lost in one's confusion without the tools for healing or self-help. Often one is a mystery to oneself, and, by definition, a person lost in this self-mystery cannot be one's psychological detective. That's *my* job. I *am* the psychological detective. Emotional intelligence is the calling card of my profession, and I am often called to sleuth through the red herrings, viable clues, and smoking guns of the psyche, to put the pieces of the puzzle of dysfunction together. Where people possess personal blind spots, I shine a spotlight designed to expose experiences, thoughts, and feelings that lead to further exploration, understanding, and ultimate change in themselves and subsequently in their relationships

LOVE AND SELF-AWARENESS

Change begins with self-awareness, including what I refer to as our Relational IQ, a subset of our general IQ. General IQ is limited to measuring a person's reasoning ability, use of information, and logic to address problems and make predictions with a certain amount of accuracy based on data. This quotient is believed to be predetermined at birth. Relational IQ, on the other hand, is our ability to explore and understand how we relate to others and adjust our behavior based on individual and social interactions. Like our general IQ, we are born with certain abilities when it comes to forming and maintaining relationships. However, I believe that our Relational IQ is mostly guided and shaped by our early formative experiences from within our families of origin. These patterns are later rehearsed, internalized, and serve as protypes for all future relationships, irrespective of whether they enhance relationships and the self or cause distress. Fortunately, I believe the unhealthy learned dynamics of relating to others and, ultimately, ourselves, can be reshaped and reconstructed through introspection. Well-guided and purposeful introspection can lead to self-awareness, and that is the first step toward building healthy relationships from the inside out.

Self-awareness is a buzzword with a plethora of books written in its honor. For our work together, and before we go any further, let's agree that we are referring to self-awareness as "the process by which one has a great conscious knowledge of one's character, feelings, motives, and desires, which leads to even greater self-awareness." To move beyond the textbook definition of self-awareness and understand its significance and importance in the journey of personal change, one must personally engage in the process of introspection previously mentioned by exploring, examining, and analyzing to gain insight into one's internal emotional and psychological workings. The long and winding road to and from self-awareness begins with getting back to the basics of love and life from within the mind.

Love is a topic too vast to cover fully in these pages, but it is the foundation of most of our significant relationships, beginning with the one we have with ourselves. How we love ourselves and others—how we were taught to love and shown love in our family of origin—are what form our Relational IQ. Of course, some people are more adept with some relationships than others: familial, platonic, romantic, and more. However, patterns of relating to others can be noted across relationships. For example, I have worked with numerous patients who have had trouble bonding with their children and their significant others. They can only reach a certain point of emotional closeness, whether the relationship is with a sibling, child, lover, or friend.

Trying to do justice to *love* is a losing battle. For our purpose, I will borrow Dr. M. Scott Peck's definition of love, as it has resonated with my work over the years as a therapist and a person who has experienced love in all its beauty and pain. Peck defines love as the extension of oneself for the sake of the other in its purest form. Love is both a noun and a verb. Most struggle with it in practice. I believe to love someone across relationships is to show them love through sharing thoughts, feelings, and actions.

Ultimately how we love is at the root of most people's relationship challenges. The mismatches between words and actions in the expression of love create a tremendous amount of friction between people.

"He doesn't love me enough. She doesn't show me love. I never learned to love. I don't love myself, so how can I love others? No one loves me. My parents never taught me love. I never experienced love. I want to be in love. I lost the love of my life. Help me find love." These are among the comments I hear as a clinician and in my personal life, as I'm sure you do as well. Love is a universal condition and language. Unfortunately, not all learn to speak the language well. For example:

Patient: "I want my wife to show me that she loves me. Or at least tell me . . . she never does."

Me: "I am sorry to hear you're feeling unloved in your relationship. Let's put that on hold for a minute. Can I ask you how you show her that you love her?"

Patient: [Silent with a clueless expression.]

It is at this place where the journey of self-awareness begins in the effort to build healthy relationships from the inside out. First and foremost, we need to become aware of how we love ourselves and others. This can only be achieved by gaining self-awareness. Without self-awareness, the changes you make will be short-term, inauthentic, faulty, cosmetic, and non-transformational. And honesty equates to self-awareness, for it is only genuine exploration of oneself that enables self-awareness. Therefore, I hope to inspire you to look within as you begin to transform your life from the inside out.

As a psychotherapist who directs and guides this kind of transformation regularly, I am often confronted by negative, repetitive patterns of dysfunction expressed through patients' symptoms as manifestations of their unhealthy relational dynamics. These challenges are not limited to romantic relationships but include familial, platonic, and other relational contexts. Although a patient may desire a different life from the one they are living, familiarity breeds comfort and safety, resulting in their feelings of "stuckness." "I can't seem to change my ways. It's the same thing in every relationship; I don't like it and feel stuck" is a confession often shared by many of my patients.

Yet change, however positive and regenerative, evokes fear and grave discomfort, which can often feel daunting and overwhelming because the unknown is always frightening and menacing. We need to acknowledge and confront our fear—the one unique emotion behind most of our reasons or excuses for not saying what we think, how we genuinely feel, and what we passionately desire to do. Fear can be debilitating and paralyzing, hindering individual and relational growth and progress. Yet as challenging as it may be to confront our fears in the hopes of giving birth to change, I believe it is in this space of fear and discomfort that metamorphosis takes place.

I know this space all too well, as I lived most of my childhood and young adulthood in this sphere of fear. It was only when I started my individual therapy as a graduate student that my personal journey of transformation began and I finally started to chip away at my fears. I believe the foundation had been set years earlier for immersing myself in self-knowledge and recognition as if I were born to be a therapist.

I know this now as a result of my transformation from

who I was then to who I am today. Yet as a psychotherapist, I should have realized then that since self-awareness generally leads to improved emotional intelligence, self-organization, and self-efficacy, it was only logical that self-knowledge would also lead to a highly bolstered Relational IQ. Being "self-aware" was a familiar concept to me theoretically, but I did not realize nor appreciate its enormous value and impact from a clinical and personal perspective. Only once I improved my personal Relational IQ did it totally transform my ability to achieve practical, concrete, sustainable, permanent results as a psychotherapist. I learned firsthand how self-awareness feeds and is the catalyst for positive change out of dysfunction from within and with those around us.

To impart worthwhile advice toward this end, allow me to share my process and part of the long and winding road of my life with you, to inspire and motivate you to take the first steps on your journey of change.

MY STORY

I come from an immigrant family, and my father always preached: "I brought you to this country so you could have opportunities I never had." If you hear that often enough, it becomes part of one's DNA. The value of education was always emphasized in my family, although for different reasons for me than for my brothers. For most of my undergraduate years, I floated around, not knowing what I wanted to pursue; who can focus on that when you have to work full time and attend school in the evening? It was challenging, but my father's voice thundered in the back of my head every time I thought I needed to drop out because the workload was too much. I could barely stay awake during class, but I had a goal and knew what I had to do to get there. If multi-tasking were a part of it, that would be the price. I knew, even though my father had disowned me at this point (I'll share more on that in the coming chapters), that I still had a desire to please him and make him proud. Somehow, I landed in the department of sociology, and it was a proud moment for me when I received my undergraduate degree from Concordia University in Montreal, Canada.

I graduated with honors despite being on academic probation for the first two years, which was a pure function of trying to do it all; something had to suffer. At that time, it was clearly my grades. As I was able to devote more time to school, I began to achieve academic excellence. Still not knowing what I wanted to pursue nor what I was destined to do, I applied to Montreal's McGill University, which, at the time, was considered the Harvard of Canada. I had very little guidance and direction with regard to programs, so I randomly chose psychology. The day I received my letter of acceptance from the Department of Educational and Counselling Psychology was one of the happiest days of my life. Now I know it was never random but my destiny to become a psychotherapist.

My years at McGill were the best of my life academically and personally. Academically I excelled and collaborated with a professor, Dr. Mark Aulls, who later became my thesis advisor, mentor, and father figure. He helped me to see the light in myself that I never even knew existed. I came to accept parts of myself that I had rejected and long hated. These years were transformative in so many ways—and little did I know there would be so much more to come.

After graduating from McGill University with excellence, I decided to pursue my passion in psychology by attending the nearby Argyle Institute, where I would have my first clinical experience with a patient and attend my therapy. My personal therapy was a prerequisite to receiving my post-master's certification and licensure.

Dr. Frank had a posh and elevated speech pattern that sometimes sounded like he was a living treatise or tome. As the author of several academic books, Dr. Frank had a mind that was of that rare, expanded variety. His lowest and common parlance could be grossly mistaken for imitation, reliance on rote memory, or even plagiaristic expressions. Yet despite the perceived flaws of his golden tongue, his was all spontaneous improvisation of a million inspirations. Turning the consummate pages of his brilliant mind in a way that was clinical yet very heart-relevant to me, I was lucky enough to read and learn from him in session and treatment.

From seeker to soul scholar, I would learn that through exploration of the past, we can reach a certain level of understanding that influences the present and helps shape the future by changing the ways we think, feel, and act. All this lighted upon me under Dr. Frank's fatherly gaze as I made my way from unconscious and dark repetition to illumination, from confusion to clarity. He helped me untangle the mystery of myself, the knot of my soul that tied me to my family-of-origin dynamics and issues, freeing me from false narratives, both conscious and unconscious, as well as the projections of negative emotions and my past.

I remember our sessions well; they replay like scenes in the theater of my mind, even today. My exploration began with investigating my conflicted relationship with my father, bicultural identity issues, and leaving home at age sixteen and its aftermath. Despite being raised in a patriarchal Indian family where I was muted most of my life, I wanted my father to know that not only had I survived, but I had but thrived in conditions and circumstances that were oppressive physically and emotionally. I was a walking example of how one can overcome life's darkest moments once one emerges out of the fog and confusion that was once their life.

I was in that confusion and fog for years, and in my darkest moments, I experienced suicidal ideations. Luckily these thoughts were fleeting. I knew I did not want to die. I only wanted to escape my life, not life itself. With the support of my mother, brothers, close friends, and mentors, I was able to see myself in a way that I thought would never be possible. I was and am a survivor and not a victim of my childhood. As a child, I had no choice, but as an adult, I knew I had the power to choose my path, and I knew that path would be a path of opportunities and a bright future that I would create for myself.

UNF*CK AWARENESS

My past did not have to be my future—a mantra I share today with my patients as I will share with you. Your past does not have to be your future. We can make choices that will lead to better outcomes; however, we need to start from within, and my journey through individual therapy was just that. It was the beginning of transforming my life by dealing with my internal negative thoughts before I could deal with the ones I projected onto the world. I had to take responsibility for my shit, as I now encourage you to do the same. It's imperative to know your emotional baggage before you attempt to join with others through relationships.

My experience with Dr. Frank helped me be the best version of myself for myself, for those around me, and most of all, for my patients. I know what it's like to sit on both sides of the couch. I have true empathy for everyone who walks into my office. I share with them, as I am sharing with you today, that the journey is difficult, as is change. However, it is possible—and I am living proof.

This is not a textbook story; this is *my* story of unf*cking me and my relationships.

What follows is a composite of vignettes of early therapy sessions with Dr. Frank. I've combined them to be succinct. Insights and breakthroughs take time and patience, but they are well worth the effort. I share my private experiences with you in hopes that it will show you a helpful vision of what it looks like to begin building healthy relationships from the inside out.

IN SESSION WITH DR. FRANK

"I don't need therapy," I began. "I am only here for didactic purposes, as it's required to graduate from the program." Blindly self-convinced, it was an attempt to calm my unconscious uncertainty and nervousness, though deep down, I knew better.

"Good to know," Dr. Frank replied. His professionally amused, soft, and polite smile made it clear he'd heard my line many times before. "Have a seat."

After I sat on the couch and explained my academic needs, Dr. Frank asked the classic question, "Tell me about yourself."

"Gosh," I said. "Where do I even start? My past, I suppose?" I coughed. "Excuse me." I tried to clear my throat. "Story of my life." I laughed nervously.

"Interesting. Do you do that every time you talk of yourself?"

"What, lose my voice?"

"Yes."

"Sometimes."

"Let's explore that. Tell me more."

I froze in fear. It had only been three minutes into the session, and already, this psychoanalytic genius had cut to the crux of my issues and the all-too-revealing symbols of them.

"Dr. Frank, you are perceptive, aren't you? Well, at times, I feel I'm a voice with no sound. Even as I speak, no sound comes out. Mine is a voice that does not speak. It never has."

"Have you always felt this way, and who do you feel took that away from you?"

I covered my face with my hands, trying in vain to hide my expression behind them, shaking my head.

Silence.

As the emotion thickened in my throat, it began to gurgle with sorrow. "My father; we have always had a very conflicted relationship from as far back as I can remember. I remember somehow always being afraid of him."

"What is the earliest memory you have of your father?"

What appeared to be on the surface a relatively easy question to answer led me to a place inside my mind and heart that I had locked up for the sake of self-preservation. The contents of my unconscious mind and all I had hidden there would eventually need to be tapped into as much as possible to resolve some of the issues. Being a psychoanalyst, a true believer in the "power of the unconscious mind to dictate our emotions and behavior," I knew what was in store with Dr. Frank. I knew that he would help me find my way ahead as I confronted my reflection. This murky self was twisted and had been tossed and turned and deformed by fate and a fury of anguish.

As I prodded my self for the greenest memory I possessed of my father, I was, as might be expected for a psychological pilgrim, unaware of how that moment when my therapist imposed his psychological flashlight would hold relevance and harbor positive repercussions for my healing. I would examine the wounds my father unknowingly and unintentionally inflicted upon me as he, too, was trying to navigate through his life the best that he could.

But I was a quick learner who would emerge from negative inertia to positive change.

There was a little hand-wringing on my part and a lot of psychological hand-holding from this very well-educated and reputable clinician who was gentle and kind but also confrontational when needed. There was no escaping him in that office, which was exactly what I needed. I had already spent too much time doing that outside of those four walls. In time, Dr. Frank would become everything I needed him to be—a flashlight, a lifeline, an active ear, a father figure, a coach, a teacher, and a mentor.

Dr. Frank led me into the heart of myself and my dysfunctions so that I might speak for myself, break the silence for the first time in my life, and come to terms with my past and my very conflicted relationship with my father and its subsequent ramifications on how I thought and felt about my place in the world.

And so I began my inner journey by telling Dr. Frank of the beginning of my outward one.

"Well," I said, "I recall the morning I was standing on the platform at Sonipat Junction railway station in India with my mother and older brother." I could still smell the lingering diesel vapor, creosoted ties, and oily brake dust mingling with the terrible odor of open sewers. It was a peaceful morning compared to most days when rickshaws and bicycles rushed through the veins and arteries that give life to India. The frightening sound of air bleeding off an idling train engine punctuated the uncanny stillness. It caused me to seek refuge behind my mother, my saving grace, my protector, my shield, my all.

"Once onboard the train, my stressed mother fell asleep instantly on my shoulder." Hearing the first snort of the engine's exhaust, I repositioned her head and looked out and down the tracks ahead, only to receive a face full of diesel smoke. But I paid no mind because a new phase of life was underway, and I was excited.

"Why do you think brings this to your mind, Anita? I believe I asked you about the earliest memory you have of your father."

"I don't know; anyway, I am getting there . . . maybe." But as I dwelled on it and explored it further, I could only answer to the memory that it must have something to do with my struggle with silence. "I guess it's relevant because, mmm, because that was when we were on our way to join my father. He didn't live with us for the early years of my life. And he infrequently visited due to his work schedule and financial limitations. From what I can recall, I saw him as an imposing man whom I didn't know very well and whom I never knew until years later when I could see him as someone other than my father, a man who had emotional and psychological challenges."

"Now we're getting somewhere," Dr. Frank said. "It's only natural for the subconscious to deflect and sidestep the actual question by providing something interesting that does not answer directly because it does not want to hear the question nor answer it to protect the self from harm in the form of stress, anxiety, and, at times, depression. Let's try again. Can you share a memory of your father? Take your time, Anita."

"Hmmm, OK, so it's related to what I shared previously about our journey from India to Germany. As I shared, I hadn't spent much time with him, so it was as if I were meeting him for the first time. I remember feeling scared and shaking and wrapping myself around my mother's leg, something I often did when he was around. Interestingly, my older brother always had a very different reaction to him. I always felt that my father loved him more because he was the firstborn son, a coveted role in Indian culture.

"Anyhow, I digress. We had traveled from quite a distance to reunite our family. All I knew about the circumstances was that he had gone to Germany to build a brighter future for us and that he was naturally a curious and adventurous person. He always wanted to see the world, as my paternal grandfather and my mother often told me. Now that I think of it, I am very much like him; I have a thirst to see the world and ask way too many questions, something he and I often sparred over.

"Getting back to that day, my father had gone to meet us at the gate, but we were nowhere in sight. He soon learned that a lady with two young children had fainted and had been taken to the hospital. That is where he found us a few hours later. My mother, a woman who had rarely traveled by car, had just crossed the ocean with her two children to a land she knew nothing about, nor did she speak the language. Can you even imagine how she felt? I don't recall much about the hospital, only that it was the first time I had ever seen my parents embrace. My mother clung to him like a log floating in the sea. Then quickly, it was all about getting us to our new home and settled. At the time, he was delighted to see us and walked us outside, where we took a taxi to the train station to begin our final leg to West Berlin."

"How does that make you feel?"

"It makes me feel . . . like . . . I sensed what the world was like even from a young age. That it's you against it, that you have to make it, or, at the very least, survive, by any means possible, by any means necessary."

"That's more like a thought stemming from a perception. Let's get even more basic. What is the emotion you relate to that memory? Happy, angry, sad, fearful, or excited?"

"I have mixed feelings—happy, sad, and confused."

"Tell me more."

"I learned early on that living in the world was complicated. I watched my parents struggle financially, but I never felt like my needs were not going to be met, and they always were. Both my parents had a solid work ethic. It was a traditional setup: my dad worked outside the home while my mother managed everything else. I know they experienced a great deal of racism in Germany. Maybe that's why my father felt he had to shove Indian culture down our throats as we tried to integrate and assimilate into mainstream German culture. He clearly wanted to maintain and preserve the traditions he grew up with."

"He wanted you to embody the traditional roles ascribed to Indian girls?"

"Absolutely! I was always told that when the time came, he would arrange my marriage and that I need not worry about that part of my life, which created the opposite effect. I lived in fear of this 'arranged marriage.' F*ck! Can you imagine? How horrible! He saw life only through the Indian lens and had limited options. That was his reality, and to believe or dream of something outside that . . ."

"In essence, the vision you had for your life clashed with his from an early age—like dating, remaining unwed, or marrying for love."

"Yes, he couldn't imagine that, nor was it ever presented as an option. There were no discussions with my father, only orders and commands, not just for us but for my mother too. She was much more open to accepting mainstream cultural norms and values, but she was not the boss, so it didn't matter. He was. The Indian way was the only way in our household."

"Do you think he feared you wouldn't make it in the world as a woman? And was that based on his feelings of whether he had made it and had achieved a certain level of success?"

"To be honest, later in his life, I think he regretted leaving India, his family, his respectful job, friends, for a life full of challenges—challenges he tried to manage alone, which I think often made him feel unsuccessful in many ways. To answer your question about me, I think he believed my success hinged on marrying well. After all, that is what his culture told him, so why would he think differently? Of course, this was a painful realization on my part. It hurt deeply and made me question my value as a woman in the world in and out of wedlock. That's part of why I felt his authority behind calling me stupid or warning me not to embarrass myself, him, and my family. I sensed the experience of a hard life and hard world lived, which was his reality, which I feared, in the final analysis, was the last, absolute, and irrefutable reality of the world, and there might be nothing beyond that.

"Early on, I wanted to be a strong, independent woman. But I felt I couldn't express any of that without being punished. Over time, I learned to tuck that away to survive my family life. It wasn't easy, as it often got untucked! Especially my views against arranged marriage, although I knew and understood the intentions behind his plan; he wanted me to be taken care of financially and maritally. I got it but didn't want it. I wanted to take care of myself and, more importantly, prove to him that I could do it! I did not want his choices to be my choices."

"Now we're getting somewhere. Continue with that memory you shared earlier. Try to focus on details, details that may trigger other thoughts and feelings. Let's see where it leads, shall we?"

"OK. As we waited for the local train to my father's apartment, I first noticed the contrast in weather compared to India. The air was crisp and dry, the sun's warmth tempered by cool breezes coming off of green mountains. It was surreal and felt like being wrapped inside a dream. When we boarded the train, I remember thinking it looked and smelled like a hospital. It was almost too clean and carried the odor of cleaning chemicals. No one spoke, and passengers had plenty of space between them. This was very different from the rough and raucous Indian railway, with smelly trains packed to the brim, passengers seated on one another's laps, and everyone using their time to socialize. My father began a discussion with my mother regarding his life in Germany. Much to her surprise, he was not as enthusiastic as she may have expected. While he admired German tenacity in business, he found it challenging to socialize and make friends or locate Indian products at the market. He continued this conversation as we walked from the West Berlin train station to his apartment. While my brother and I were astonished by this concrete jungle, my father was clearly disappointed, as was my mother upon learning of his negative experiences."

"You say he had difficulty socializing and integrating into German culture. Tell me more about this."

"From what I gathered from my parents' conversations, it was related to being a foreigner and minority in a country once known for its beliefs in a master race. Apparently, he experienced a great deal of racism. I felt bad for him because he worked so hard and sacrificed so much to provide for us."

I stopped talking for a moment as my eyes welled up. "Oh, my father, he had the strongest work ethic, could be loving at times, and had the worst temper. He was so complicated and conflicted. I hated him and loved him." I continued to cry.

Dr. Frank consoled me with his eyes, although I would have preferred a fatherly hug, something I longed for but also feared. "Do you think he was a beaten-down man then, Anita?"

I sobbed and nodded.

"Please continue when you're ready. It's OK. I am here with you."

"Well, as the months passed, it became evident that my

parents were finding it more and more difficult to make friends and integrate into German culture. My father started talking about moving us to a different country. To be honest, we all missed the gatherings we had in India with our extended family. Although I had and still have many grievances with Indian culture, I do value its traditions around food and family. If not daily, then weekly, we would come together with extended family members to share meals. I enjoyed observing my parents engaging in conversations while I mingled with my cousins. On these occasions, my father seemed happy, which made me happy and less frightened of him. Another reason my father thought it best to leave Germany was that the laws required him to renew his immigration papers yearly. Clearly, the political situation was not welcoming to foreigners, and this uncertainty kept my father on edge. So after much contemplation, my father decided that it was time to leave Germany and settle in a nation with friendly immigration policies.

"Through much investigation, my father learned that Canada was friendly to foreigners and had an immigration policy that would secure our future permanently. Soon after, he went to the Canadian embassy in Berlin to get the ball rolling. As the story goes, while standing in line waiting to be attended to, he asked the person in front of him, 'What is the best city in Canada to live in?' 'Montreal' was the response. So just like that, we packed our bags and, at the suggestion of a stranger, moved to Montreal. That spontaneity, throwing caution to the wind and taking action, was a significant part of my father's personality, the part that I admired the most and fondly look back on today with the realization that I am more like him than I once believed.

"When we arrived in Canada and cleared immigration, my father's gumption was something to behold. He went directly to a telephone booth and looked for my mother's maiden family name. Last names connect people: especially in the Indian culture, they convey critical information about that person's religion, caste, and region in which they lived. He hoped a connection would help us settle into this new city and country. We knew no one and only had our personal belongings in hand. Lucky for us, a family he called responded well to our story of migration and, just like that, invited us to stay as long as needed. Later we learned that although we were not directly related, we did discover some family ties. We stayed with them until my father could secure employment and get established. To this day, I remain in sheer amazement that a random person decided my fate by suggesting Montreal to my father."

"That's an amazing story, Anita. It illustrates some of the qualities I see in you. And yes, you're more like your father than you think. That's a good thing! Reconciling the love and hate you felt and feel from him even today is difficult. However, I believe it's better than indifference. It means you care and are conflicted. That's OK! We will work through these emotions together. And might I add that although 'hate' is a strong word, it's normal to feel that about people we love, especially parents. Just remember, the flip side of that coin is love.

"We're making a lot of headway today, and I am proud of you and admire you for staying true and committed to your mental health. Not only personally but also professionally. If you're going to be an effective therapist, it's imperative that you work through your personal psychosocial history and experience firsthand what it is like to be sitting where you are today, with all that you are thinking and feeling. I admire you."

"Thank you, Dr. Frank. That means a lot coming from you. I appreciate you sharing that with me."

And just like that, his kind and gentle smile put me at ease and gave me the strength and support I needed to continue my story.

"Within a short time, my father secured a job as a machinist with General Electric, which enabled us to move into our apartment—a big relief to my parents. Although we were grateful to our host family, it was time to establish ourselves. Despite being relieved to be gainfully employed, I knew deep down my father felt he had accepted a position below his qualifications, damaging his ego. Yet he knew he had no other choice with a wife and family in tow. He would later retire from GE with over twenty-five years of service.

"To satisfy his cravings and pay homage to his familial lineage of goldsmith entrepreneurs, he decided to rent a stall at the local flea market for Sundays. I could tell he enjoyed the wheeling and dealing he had so loved in India. It reminded him of his family, particularly his brothers back home, and gave him the opportunity to connect with people other than his work colleagues and make a little extra money. I also think it brought my parents closer; it was one of the few times I watched them collaborate and spend time together that was not solely devoted to the family and us. I was impressed with his incredible work ethic and interest in returning to his entrepreneurial roots.

"After many years of working at GE and the flea market on Sundays, I noticed he was becoming increasingly dissatisfied with life. With age, he was becoming increasingly conscious of his change in socioeconomic status from India to Canada, which manifested as anger that was targeted toward us, including my mother. This made life at home unbearable. In addition, I knew he was under constant pressure from his family in India to sponsor their migration to Canada. Although he wanted to help them, he was very concerned about the lifestyle adjustment they would have to make, as he did, only to be dissatisfied. Perhaps he was projecting his emotional experience and feelings of regret onto them. Anyhow, I remember my parents fighting a great deal over this issue and the many battles I was aware of between him and his brothers in India. They often taunted him about the fabulous life he was living, a view cultivated by him without informing them of the sacrifices he had made along the way. They always resented him for this, and he always resented them for adding more conflict to his life."

"Sounds like he faced a great deal of pressure trying to meet not only the financial demands of his family but also everyone else back home. That's a tremendous amount of stress for one person, Anita."

"Yes, it was, and believe me, I paid the price for it. Every time he was mad at them, he was mad at me, and I had nothing to do with it. On top of that, I had to be the perfect little

Indian girl. I had pressure, too, Dr. Frank. Let's not forget that I had to try to be something I wasn't."

"I am sorry you're feeling that I am not being sympathetic to you, Anita. I was merely validating what you said yourself. And I appreciate your challenges of growing up in two opposing cultures and how difficult that must have been for you."

"I am sorry, Dr. Frank; I don't know why your comment upset me. I guess all my life, my voice hasn't been heard, and it felt like you were doing that just now when you validated his experience over mine. Oh, my god, why am I so f*cked up and why is this so hard? You're just trying to help me."

"It's OK, I am not upset with you, and I am glad you feel safe enough with me to share your feelings of frustration, not only about your father but this process, about my response. It tells me that you trust me and that we are making progress."

"Thank you for understanding and accepting me, even the frustrated and angry me. My father never did. Clearly, you do and I appreciate that about you and this process.

"OK, so my father struggled with integrating into mainstream culture, unlike my mother. Although at times it appeared he did to the outside world, he did not! He strictly maintained Indian cultural norms and values. And although Indian culture had changed and evolved since he lived there, he had not. Even by Indian standards, his views on some things were dated. As you can imagine, this created daily challenges for me. We disagreed about nearly everything. I wasn't even allowed to wear a dress or a skirt because my father thought they were provocative! I had to wear dress pants. All this sounds shallow, but it was just the tip of the iceberg, an iceberg that I thought would eventually sink me. As I grew older, I experienced the emotional and psychological struggles of living in two vastly opposing cultures. Despite my challenges and our battles, I remained respectful of his courage, ingenuity, industriousness, and commitment to our family. Again, it was about reconciling my love and hate for him. And I know that most teens go through these challenges; however, mine was a two-faced monster."

"Anita, I am sorry you had to go through that as a teenager, but I feel like you've skipped aspects of your childhood. Can you tell me more about your early years in India, if you can remember that far back, and how you felt? This will help me to understand your familial landscape better."

"OK. Wow. I'll try. Let's see. Mmm. What is there to say but that I was a very shy little girl who often hid behind her mother among adults. I have a vague memory of peeing my pants while wrapped around my mother's leg while being scolded by my father. I can see myself now; I was wearing a white dress made by my mother, and then I was urinating. That's it! I guess that says it all! I was a little girl who feared her father and his temper. However, when he wasn't around, I was a happy child and spent a great deal of time with my older brother, cousins, and extended family members. It's customary, or was then anyway, that the bride moves in with her husband's family after marriage. Until immigrating to Germany, we lived with my paternal grandparents and uncles, even after my father left for Germany. Much of what I remember is based on some early memories, pictures, and my mother's stories. She says that I was an easygoing little girl and self-sufficient from the get-go."

"You didn't have any perception that anything was missing? You didn't miss your father?"

"Not that I can remember. Don't forget I was surrounded by extended family. I think at times, I forgot that he even existed because I was very close to my uncle, my father's younger brother. I guess he filled that void. I do recall feeling confused when my father did visit."

"How did you feel confused, Anita?"

I paused. "This is going to sound weird. I remember my mother explaining to me very clearly who my father was and reminding me that he was off doing great things for us in other countries for our welfare. I guess if she felt compelled to do that, then she must have been worried that I would forget him? I presume so. She explained that my father, above all, higher than any love, was a provider, which in its way and sense, was the greatest love of all. According to her, it was the love of doing, put into action, and not love merely spoken. It was the love proof of sweat and labor. And she tenderly called our family and me my father's 'labor of love.'"

"Interesting. I sense that you were proud of him?"

"Yes, mostly because seeing little girls in the streets begging for food and shelter as I shopped with my mother further validated my mom's story of why he was absent."

"So your primary years were spent with your father's family. Tell me more about them. This will give me a window into your father's life."

"Well, my father's family, by Indian standards, were wealthy, categorized as Rajputs, who are from the ruling warrior caste of India. Caste dictates almost every aspect of Hindu religious and social life, trapping people into fixed social orders from which it's impossible to escape. It was the first thing I remember learning about my heritage. They were goldsmiths who established and operated a handcrafted jewelry business. My one uncle took over the family business while another studied medicine, and my father was the only one who had the hunger to travel and took a completely different path. To pursue his passion for travel, he secured employment as a health inspector on the Indian railways. From what my mother tells and later conversations with him, he loved the job. It allowed him to travel all over India with very little cost."

"Sounds like he was on a mission."

"Yes. I remember my mother telling my brother and me about our father's journey to Berlin. She held my tiny hand so tightly that I wasn't sure if it was more important for her to tell us the story or tell it to herself again. As she recounted the details of when our father took his first trip to Germany, her anxiety seemed to rise, and sweat began to bead on her forehead. She explained to us that it was difficult for anyone to leave India. Even though my father did not have enough money to travel by air, he was determined to find a way there. To compound matters, the Indian government limited the amount of money one can take out of the country to the equivalent of fifty United States dollars. She said nothing could stop my father from pursuing his objectives, so he improvised a plan to get to Europe by taking a cargo ship across the Arabian Sea to Pakistan. Inside his belongings, he was careful to pack a bar of soap. Before he boarded, he cut the soap in half, hollowed it out, hid some money in the cavity, then rejoined the two halves by lathering up the soap and letting it dry. He was successful in getting it past the authorities when boarding the ship. Once out at sea, he used the money to buy alcohol. He knew that Pakistan was under strict prohibition. So when they docked in Pakistan, he sold the alcohol at a profit to several eager Pakistanis. Using his earnings, he took a train from Pakistan to Europe, eventually getting him into West Berlin. And this is where he would plant the seeds to start the next chapter of our lives. As nervous as my mother appeared, it was clear she was proud to share this important story of our father's ingenuity with us."

"Your father was very creative, not to mention resourceful; remind you of anyone?"

"Thank you, Dr. Frank. Yup, the more I share about him, the more I realize how similar we are. Maybe that's why we butt heads so often. Similar yet very different. Is that possible?"

"Clearly, it is. And yes, similar personalities tend to clash. Do you remember when all this clashing started between you and him?"

"Interesting question. I felt we had always clashed, but I guess that's not true. Let me see . . . I don't . . . well, I recall the first day of the festival of Holi. I recall the market very vividly, almost as if it were yesterday."

"What made you think of the market in relation to the

conflict with your father? How are the two connected?"

"I'm not sure."

"That's OK; please continue. In time, the relationship between the two will be revealed as your conscious mind meets with your unconscious mind."

"Don't get all Freudian on me, Dr. Frank. Sorry, OK, it's what you do. Let me think. As a little girl, I found the market to be a stressful place, although now I think they are rather beautiful and fascinating. Hmm. I saw the rickshaws whizzing about with poor Indian boys pedaling their lives away, bicycle couriers, people haggling over goods and services, people buying and selling, coming and going. I saw it all as a kind of circus. My mother often reminds me of this today: how the market would make me very nervous as a little girl."

"What kinds of feelings are being triggered right now as you share this story?"

"I guess fear. I feared the commerce of the world, felt like it was all a bunch of people who had to grow up—who had been forced to grow up, whether they'd had a proper childhood or not. Grown-ups. The more I think of it, the more it makes sense to me now. Those markets are filled with children taking on adult roles, working when they should be enjoying their childhood but that's clearly not an option for them."

"Like your father, you mean. He never had an option other than being an adult like those children at the market, and from what you've told me, you were in many ways a parentified child yourself. Hence the connection between the market and the conflict between you and your father. He didn't allow you to be a child either. The beginning of your conflict, perhaps?"

"Wow, that's quite the interpretation, Dr. Frank, and I think pretty accurate. As a little girl, I remember shopping with my father and picking up a toy and him saying, 'Put that back, toys are for children, and you're not a child.' I remember thinking, 'But I *am!*' How sad is that?"

"Your father was a parentified child, and he parentified you at a very early age."

"Yup, it's not his fault. He was only doing what he knew how to do."

"Anita, as I have said before, we are not here to blame him or anyone. Rather, our purpose is to explore, understand, and create change, which can't be achieved without self-awareness through introspection."

"You're right, thank you. I needed to hear that. And having come to this awareness I will never do this to my children. Children need to be children, not mini-adults. Getting back to my father, although being the firstborn son is a coveted role in the Indian culture, it is not without burdens and pressure. My father's fate had been sealed by birth order, gender, and cultural expectations! So as I see it, it was inevitable that he fell into an unfeeling hole, at times struggled with mental health, and his relationships suffered. My father was like many men who suffer alone. They self-medicate through alcohol and substance abuse to cope and mask their pain.

"Now that I think of it, he was like those people I saw at the marketplace, or rather what I saw going on behind them. As their faces fell, their humanity cried out to be healed from the relational, marital, and familial problems. Even as a little girl, I knew there was something to that. The adults seemed dulled by taking the edge off, numbed, emotionless, like life and the world had beaten the best and sweetest part out of them, beaten out of them the inner life that makes you alive, like . . . it wasn't important or even relevant anymore. The only thing that mattered was making money, subsisting, and surviving in this challenging world. You add children to that equation, what do you get? Me, Anita. You get me and my father and the problems we had."

"You sensed, as a child, that people forget to be human by the mechanism of trying to make ends meet and survive in the world?"

"Yes, I remember the feelings and thoughts but didn't have the language to express it or even make sense of it. Now I do. It tingled and hurt my heart and made me sad at times. Now I know why. And that was related, in my mind somehow, to trying to forget about having to do anything with my father or the absence that I knew to miss, because of it. Somehow those two things are intertwined."

"That must have been difficult for you, Anita."

"It was. But as I said, I didn't know what I didn't know but only what I felt, if that makes sense. Can I share a happy memory? I do have those too! All I've done is talk about all the bad stuff. There were good times!"

"Of course you can, and please do."

"Despite what I said about the market, I have this incredible memory. On this particular day, both my parents had taken us to the market. My mother was focused on getting supplies while my father told us about the first day of Holi, the festival of color. He wanted us to learn about Indian holidays, traditions, and customs. Holi marks the beginning of spring after a long winter in a symbolic triumph of good over evil. Even then, that resonated in my child's heart with the sick feeling of my one day having to be in the world, to be an insensate, half-smiling, numbed clown. Within a matter of seconds, we found ourselves blanketed in glorious color and the embrace of joyous Indians. Somehow, through the tidal wave of undulating bodies and the sting of powder in her eyes, my mother found the reserve to drag us to buy supplies.

"As we made our way to the vendor, the festivities had grown old. Like life had for most adults, who were coming and going as if the celebration rang as a hollow formality that seemed silly, a large cloud of colorful dust rose to paint our faces in red, green, and yellow. We looked at one another with some concern but then began laughing uncontrollably. Perhaps it was the release of my mother's anxiety or our exhaustion from the humidity that spurred our laughter.

"The same day, years later, marked the beginning of our journey of migration from India to Frankfurt to reunite with my father. Looking back on this moment, I now see it as fate. After all, Holi marks a new beginning. And maybe, just maybe, we were genuinely excited to embark on this blossoming adventure together."

"Thank you for sharing this side of your father. I agree that all too often, people portray others as one-dimensional, and, of course, we are not, as you know. How wonderful to learn of this aspect of your father! It pleases me to know that you shared in some tender moments. Interesting. I'm starting to get a clearer picture of your childhood and how the difficulty of being in the world relates to the problems you had with him, which may also be the saving grace to your contextualizing him as an unintentional oppressor who was himself caught up in the rat race of existence. In his way, he wanted the best for you because he was afraid you wouldn't be able to survive in the world, given the caste system of India or the racism and push-back to success and prosperity he encountered in Germany and the world, by and large."

Dr. Frank had a warm smile on his face. I felt that he cared about me and my journey through this highly intense process called therapy. He demonstrated that he was indeed human and not just a technician of the trade. It was a heartfelt moment. I held back the tears.

"Mmm, hmm," was all I could muster to say because I felt naked and exposed. And on that note the session came to an end.

* * *

For the entire week following my first session, I felt positive and energized. I finally had someone in my life who was beginning to understand my internal workings as I was beginning to understand them myself. With each session, I would learn that my professional and personal growth hinged on self-awareness through the journey of introspection. I knew that to help my patients, I first had to help myself from the inside out.

Then came a session with Dr. Frank that was more difficult than anticipated. I had had a terrible dream about my father, as I sometimes did. Since commencing therapy, these dreams were becoming more frequent and intense.

"What's on your mind, Anita? You look rather distressed, or am I reading you wrong?"

"No, you're right. It seems that since I have been seeing you, I have started to have more dreams about my father—and not good ones. This self-awareness doesn't always feel good; I have to be honest. All I know is that I wake up feeling upset. And I can't help but blame the therapy."

"Anita, as you know yourself from your training, therapy is not the culprit here. Talking about some of these things only wakens your unconscious mind. This awakening facilitates the dripping of your unconscious thoughts and feelings into consciousness. I am not going to lecture you on dream analysis because I know you are learning all about that at the Argyle. However, I would like to know more about these dreams and the thoughts and feelings triggered by them."

"Well, it's nothing new, Dr. Frank. It's just history repeating itself in my mind's eye. My father and I are fighting, fighting, and fighting. My voice is muted; his is amplified."

"I see; the theme is of conflict, clearly. Would you mind sharing the earliest memory you have of a fight with your father?"

"I don't know if I can remember that far."

"Because you've repressed it or because it's too painful to talk about and you don't want to betray him?"

"I don't know. Maybe all the above, Dr. Frank?"

He furrowed his brow deep in thought as the wheels were turning. "Hmm. Curious."

"What?"

"It's interesting that you have shared so much about your past thus far, but you resist this process regarding any real, tell-tale conflict. Tell me whatever comes to mind."

"What are you talking about, Dr. Frank? I have shared so much; is it not good enough for you?"

"Anita, you're an intelligent woman and studying this profession; you know exactly what I am referring to. Please don't take this as an attack."

I sensed that the subconscious game was afoot! And he was right. I was being defensive because I felt attacked, a feeling I often experienced with my father.

The past flooded me with wintry breath.

"I remember . . . Montreal. My father's cold, icy grip on my life. Silence, and then speaking, but no sound would come out."

"Go on."

It started to come back to me, little by little.

"Having come from a hot country, the winters in Canada were particularly brutal for my parents. I often heard them grumbling about it, as if that would change anything. Like the once-innocent dynamic of my relationship with my father, what was once soft, harmless, fluffy powder had become a dangerous, icy crust. I'd traverse this glassy shell with great caution, but on occasion, my foot would pierce the ice, and I'd find myself knee-deep in trouble.

"When I turned sixteen, this was also how I felt at home. I did everything I could to avoid having a conversation with my father because our dialogue would invariably spiral downward into the same oppressive topics. On the other hand, my brothers were the lords of summer despite their issues with my father. It didn't matter that one was ten years younger. He was given the same license as my older brother, who was one-and-a-half years my senior. Sandwiched between them, life served me an unfair, nightmare hand, as they savored and relished the liberties showered on them, all courtesy and compliments of the broken, gender-biased system and blind spots that were the irrational and illogical traditions of Indian culture. I was its prisoner and priestess, religiously sacrificed at the altar of arranged marriage and silent partner in the forced abetting of the process of enculturation.

"Whereas my brothers were golden in their autonomy and self-governance, often, even as my father's fullhearted and open acceptance of their gender-based freedoms turned on the head of a rupee to the contrasting stricture and oppression of my glass cage, the lack of logic and cruelty never registered for him. Even as he pranced the beauty of their independence in my face, I tried to point out that inequality, injustice, and iniquity. Yet my opinions were shut down before I could even finish a sentence. Each passing day found me feeling more and more inadequate. My father expected me to understand my position as his daughter and accept my fate in an arranged marriage. I had no voice. While my father was unable to provide any kind of moral support, I was slowly suffocating."

"Let's go back a little. Tell me more about your teen years and feeling like you had no voice."

"Well, as I catapulted into my teens, I naturally began to find my voice. But it was a voice I kept mostly to myself in our home. I learned over time that my voice was not respected and not welcomed in my patriarchal household. Each time I tried, my father shut me down, and it was taken away, just like that! I did occasionally vent to my mother about my challenges with my father's myopic beliefs, but there was not much she could do other than listen, be supportive, and hug me. So she nurtured my thoughts and emotions while at the same time keeping my father from losing his shit.

"I appreciated all of that, but it felt short of what I needed, which was for her to stand up to him on my behalf or even on her behalf. I wanted her to find her voice, but I knew that wouldn't happen, nor would it change anything. She was as powerless to him as I was—so I thought; I learned differently years later. But the more I was exposed to Western society, the less effective her mediation would become."

"Your mother's perceived weakness at the time must have created more tension between the two of you."

"Yes, it did, Dr. Frank. But I worked hard at keeping those feelings at bay. I did not need to add more conflict to her life. She had enough shit to deal with.

"Whether fueled by a spike in my hormones or simply my

awakening mind, I would eventually find the courage to square off with my father face-to-face on a regular basis, which created a great deal of tension in our household. It was during these heated arguments that I first began to formulate my earliest thoughts about my father's behavior and its profound effect on those caught in his never-ending whirlwind. I was subconsciously rejecting the patriarchal culture in which I was raised. The more independent my thoughts and feelings became, the more I felt like a square peg forced into a round hole. My mind was expanding, and my appetite for alternative thinking was taking hold. I was finding my voice, or so I thought, even as it was being taken away, sound by sound, word by word, and thought by thought.

"Reflecting on this today, the constant fluctuation between my father's emotional highs and lows was a roller coaster that I find fascinating. It not only confounded me but also encouraged me to look at his behavior outside of his role as father. Clearly, he was suffering emotionally."

"Anita, you have this awareness now and perhaps had some idea back then. But you were just a teenager; it wasn't your job to care for his mental health or your parents' relationship. Again, you were a parentified child when you just needed to be a child. Do you see that?"

"I do now! It was so f*cked up! This self-awareness stuff hurts. I love it and hate it. But I appreciate its importance and relevance in my growth and building healthy relationships—not just with my parents but with everyone around me. Our family of origin is where we learn to have relationships—not always a good thing!"

"I agree, not always a good thing. But it doesn't mean good things cannot come from those experiences. If we can become aware of the things that did not work, then we can always become aware of things that *do* work and our role in both. And might I add that some of the experiences you've shared are a function of dealing with bicultural identity challenges? We have talked about this before but maybe not in such specific terms. When one is forced to live in two cultures, it works well when both cultures are similar and compatible but creates much conflict, as you know, when they are opposing, as in your situation."

"You're right. That was basically at the root of most of my conflict with my father. He didn't want to accept my mainstream cultural norms, and I didn't want to accept his Indian norms and values. He was trying to retain his cultural heritage, and I was doing my best to reject it.

"This double-bind started to take a toll on my mental health and his. I felt easily embarrassed by things, as most teens do; however, I had the added stress of trying to fit into two different cultures. I often felt like I didn't fit into either one. Sometimes I felt I was betraying one identity at the other's expense. Over time, these thoughts and feelings manifested as stress, anxiety, depression, and isolation."

"Tell me more about your day-to-day challenges of living in these two cultures."

"None of my friends could relate, which made things worse. I lived in mainstream culture from 8 a.m. to 3 p.m., then quickly switched to Indian culture when confronted with my father. My mother didn't care, as she was very accepting of mainstream cultural values and had integrated well, which gave me some respite. But that didn't matter much because she was not the boss. He was. I had to do stupid things to navigate this bind, which might seem insignificant now, but back then they were not!"

"Anita, I am not minimizing what you had to do to reconcile the two opposing forces in your life, by any means."

"Thank you, Dr. Frank. High school was the worst. When arriving in the mornings, I would make a beeline for the bathroom, where I'd change my clothes, put on more makeup, apply hairspray, and do whatever else I needed to do to integrate with my friends. After school, I would adjust myself accordingly if my father confronted me at home. My saving grace was that my father worked the late shift from 3 p.m. to 11 p.m., so sometimes I would miss him, but other times not! I had to be prepared for the worst-case scenario; otherwise, it would not end well. Consequently, I spent most of my early years hiding in my room because I feared my father's cruel tongue, which rolled out very mean and negative comments about my appearance and, at times, my intellect. Basically, I felt like I was living a double life. I think we were all struggling in our ways and had different coping mechanisms. My mother cooked and cleaned all day; my brothers did whatever it was that boys did and also practiced their type of hiding. My older brother immersed himself in music and played guitar, while my younger brother played a lot of tennis and street hockey. And I guess my father escaped his issues by drinking."

"Was the drinking an issue?"

"Looking back, I don't think he was an alcoholic; rather, he used it to self-medicate."

"Did your mother show concern and do something?"

"Of course, she did. But my father never listened to her or anyone else. There were nights when she would hide his bottle or even empty it in the sink. This only led to increased conflict between them, then us. He was clearly depressed at the time, but of course, it manifested in anger. Using alcohol was his coping mechanism. It didn't help that he had issues at work throughout my high school years. Nothing to do with performance but problems being laid off. I can only imagine the stress created by being the only breadwinner in the family. Financial instability only served to increase his drinking. The more he drank, the more we fought, and the more we fought, the more he drank."

"Sounds like he and your family were caught in a negative feedback loop."

"Yes, we were. We didn't know it at the time. Consequently, his health began to suffer; he was diagnosed with diabetes, was gaining weight, and was overall mentally and physically unhealthy. His drinking habits were such that by the time he finished one drink, he was on to another. Over time, we all learned the pattern and unconsciously played into the unhealthy dynamic. I know that now, but I was clueless back then."

"How would you know? You were just a child, and your mother was trying to keep her family together by doing whatever she could to keep the peace."

"So true, Dr. Frank; she tried everything. But sooner

or later, it all went to shit! He knew how to clear the room. His sharp words always harpooned me in the chest: 'Don't say anything because you'll probably say something stupid,' was a phrase I became accustomed to hearing. As a kid, if you hear that often enough, you come to believe it. Sadly, I did."

"I am sorry, Anita; no one should become accustomed to such words."

"Thank you. Unfortunately, I grew up with that statement living rent-free in my head for most of my young-adult years. These words damaged my evolving ego, which later became real hurt—the type of hurt that causes a person to shut down emotionally, question their self-worth, and lose any or all confidence. Ultimately, though, it became an essential part of the fuel I used to propel my personal development. I chose to take that negative and turn it into something useful."

"Sounds like you chose to reframe it without even knowing what that meant."

"Yes, I did, and thank god for that. I think I have always been a resilient person. Would you agree, Dr. Frank?"

"I would, happily, agree on that. Please continue."

"Well, these challenges ultimately motivated me to be better and do better. It took a while, and I am still working on it. Despite everything, I don't blame my father. I believe he did the best he could with how he was equipped."

"As I have said before, we are not here to blame, only to explore, understand, and cocreate a different reality for you— one that will enable you to free yourself from your past and live life on your terms."

"True. Isn't that what we all want? Isn't that why people come to see a therapist?"

"That's right, Anita. I am glad you're beginning to see the bigger picture. Let's move forward; having grown up in this type of environment and being a witness to your parents' clearly challenging relationship, how did this impact your ability to form relationships outside your family, in school, and at work? What was your school life like?"

"Well, I didn't always have bad grades as a child. I started out like any little girl who went to school, wanting to follow the rules, do as I was told, and please my teachers, friends, and, of course, my parents. It was easy at first but became progressively more difficult. I had a hard time focusing on school as the stress from my home life, particularly the conflict with my father, started leaking into my academic world."

"Did your mother notice, and what did she do about it? You don't mention her much."

"That's because there isn't much to say other than she tried her best and overcompensated for my father. She has always been the calming force in my life and for my brothers. She tried to shield us from my father's temper, but there was only so much she could do. She was loving and supportive in every way.

"The only real tension I had with her was my impatience with her ability to tolerate my father's belligerence toward her. I often told her to leave him. I wanted her to leave him, but not, I guess. I guess what I wanted was a display of empowerment from her. Later I realized that what I perceived as her weakness, her need to preserve the family, was perhaps a strength. I am still conflicted to some degree about that today.

"Getting back to your question, eventually my grades started to suffer, but my social life at school didn't. I was always able to make and maintain friendships. I was often sent to the principal's office for talking too much in class. I guess I was making up for all the talking I couldn't do at home. Dr. Frank, I am a rebel at heart. Always have been and always will be. Just who I am. Early in my life, I was forced to squash that side of me. Perhaps it's a function of that. Today I embrace it."

"Yes, I can see the rebel in you, Anita, and like it. It makes you who you are. Please continue."

"I was often scolded and punished by my father for my poor performance in school, but he failed to understand the cause. How can anyone thrive intellectually when they are being browbeaten mentally, day in and day out? I grew up thinking and believing that my sole purpose in life was to wed a preselected husband and procreate. There was no room for what I wanted or dreamed of, so I kind of gave up on school academically and focused on my friends."

"You were doing the best with what you had. Did those relationships include boys?"

"I tried, and no. It was made clear to me from a very young age that I was not allowed to date—only marry. 'Nice Indian girls don't date' was a mantra drilled into my head since birth. I wanted to date, attend the high school dances, and do what all my other friends were doing. But I feared my father would learn of it and I would be punished severely. Boys were

71

not even permitted to call my house. It was tough. I had to squash my emerging sexuality.

"Nearing the end of high school, the psychological and sometimes physical abuse I suffered at my father's hands began to take a toll as never before. My friends had some idea of my issues at home, but I kept most of it to myself because I felt ashamed and embarrassed. As all kids do, I often threw him under the bus while protecting him. After all, he was still my father."

"Reconciling your feelings of love and hate for him began early."

"I guess so. Although I didn't see it that way at the time, I felt the effects of it. I often struggled to hold on emotionally, psychologically, and physically. My mother and friends managed to keep me somewhat steady, but I needed more.

"Adding to the growing tension internally and externally, my father's way of dealing with my emerging sexuality only exasperated the situation. He saw threatening me with an arranged marriage as a way of taming me, which had the opposite effect. The more he spoke of it, the more distant and angrier I became. I wanted nothing to do with him or marriage. What sixteen-year-old would? Maybe in India, yes, but not in Canada, not with me."

I sat in silence for a few minutes and tried to hide my tears. Dr. Frank noticed.

"You are getting teary-eyed. What are you not saying, Anita?"

"I don't even know where to start with this one. It's f*cked-up thinking! Sorry for using the F word. I don't mean to be disrespectful. I know I have used it often in session and have felt bad after but swearing is something I grew up with. My father used profanity on a regular basis. I hope you're not offended."

"Not at all, Anita; context is everything, and you seem to use it well," he said with a smirk!

"Thank you, Dr. Frank. I try to always keep the context in mind." We both shared a laugh and a short-lived smile and continued.

"OK, so getting back to what we were talking about before . . . Dr. Frank, I am not sure if you know this or not, but Indian people are colorists in the worst way!"

"What do you mean, Anita? Please explain."

"Well, I am sure you're familiar with the term *colorism* within racism. In Indian culture, like other cultures, dark skin is considered unattractive. Indian people have a big hang-up about their shades of brown. Seriously! It's disgusting! For all my life, my father's nickname for me was *Kali*. Do you know what that means, Dr. Frank?"

"I do not."

"The direct translation from Hindi to English is 'blackie.' Oh, God, this is painful to share. My father and most of his relatives back home would openly discuss the difficulties my father would have in arranging my marriage due to my very dark skin. 'If Anita was lighter-skinned, we would have no trouble arranging her marriage.' Can you imagine hearing that about yourself? So not only did I feel completely inadequate intellectually but also physically. I was too dark to be considered pretty. This was devasting for my ego! My father thought my nickname was funny. I, however, did not and was damaged by it for years. I wore makeup that was two shades lighter than my skin to appear whiter. Pathetic, right?"

"It's not pathetic, Anita, and I am sorry you had to go through that. And it's OK; no need to hold back those tears. Your feelings of hurt are safe with me."

I sat there and wept for a good five minutes before putting myself back together to continue the session. It felt good to let it out and finally share these hurt feelings so I could be free of them.

"Dr. Frank, I don't want to talk about this anymore. Can we please move on?"

"Of course; thank you for sharing, Anita. I know that was difficult for you."

"Thank you. Moving on! I knew that I needed to decompress from all the stress in my life, and I got to a point where I had to do something to escape my circumstances. I thought that if I got a job, my father would let me go out because he's a hardworking man, and he'd respect that I wanted to work. I applied at a local fast-food restaurant, only one bus stop away. I remember it like it was yesterday. The manager was super sweet. He said, 'Well, you don't have any experience, but you are kind of cute. So, you're hired.' His response boosted my self-esteem because I thought I was too dark. As I said, according to people in India, I wasn't that pretty and nobody was going to marry me. As a teenager, I felt a great deal of worthlessness with this narrative running through my head. I was inadequate, ugly, and had no voice. Nevertheless, having a job allowed me to escape my home life. Anytime I wanted to leave the house, I would just lie to my father and tell him I had to go to work. Over time this became increasingly difficult; I was telling more lies than truths, which was not OK. I felt conflicted and guilty for just wanting to be like everyone else."

"Anita, the job and school helped you escape your home life, but it didn't change the narrative about you to yourself."

"You're right, Dr. Frank. I never thought of it that way. These were all Band-Aid approaches. My respites were temporary; I always knew I would have to return home. The tension between my father grew because, although he respected my work, he didn't like the autonomy that came with that. Rather than make me feel safe, as fathers should do, he made me scared of the world and my future. 'You have no idea what's waiting for you out there, in the wide world, do you, Anita?' Who says that to their kid? That's so f*cked up.

"I remember often tossing and turning in my bed, swimming in the burning fires of my mind, as these thoughts tortured me. There was no escape; I saw no way out of this. The future looked bleak. Although I did not want to die, at times, I sometimes thought it might be easier. These darker thoughts forced me to seek validation outside my home—a way out, a pleasant release that could restore my sense of peace and normalcy. I started spending more time with my friends, at work and school."

"Did you share your suicidal ideations with anyone?"

I took a moment before answering. "Yes, with my mother. She was very supportive and loving and remained hopeful that things would get better. She reminded me that death was not the solution. But I think she knew I didn't want to die, just escape my misery. Things would improve for short periods, but then the pattern would repeat. All honeymoons come to an end."

"Yes, they do, Anita. It sounds like your mother was your grounding force, although I know you struggled with some of her choices regarding her relationship with your father."

"She was and still is today. Anyway, all that seemed important to my father was that I marry. He feared my sexuality would get the best of me. I lived under this threat of being married to a strange Indian man that hung over my head like a noose. I feared that it would come true and that my life would be over. Sorry, Dr. Frank, I am not trying to be dramatic. As a result, I became fearful of men when it came to love. I had never gone on a date. Maybe it was best that way; my negative associations about my dark skin made me feel ugly, inadequate, and awkward."

"Of course you feared relationships with men, Anita. You never had a loving relationship with your father, the first man in your life. Fathers serve as prototypes for all future male relationships with their daughters. When we don't get what we need from our parents, we search for others to fill those roles. It's human nature. Since you were not getting the love that you needed from your father, did you find surrogates?"

Silence. "Yes." More silence. "I don't want to talk about it just yet."

"You're safe here, but I know you need time to . . . to trust my words and feel safe. When you're ready, tell me what you've been waiting to say for some time now."

UNF*CK AWARENESS

* * *

It took twenty more sessions to get me to open up to the genius of that surgical incision, that gentle, still, small probing with a potential breakthrough; to let that lost voice, which desperately wanted to speak but couldn't somehow, get it all out into the open, where my conscious mind could hear what unconsciously I wanted to say to myself all these years.

Whenever Dr. Frank and I returned to that issue of the lost voice, I began to cough and choke. As he gave me that tender fatherly gaze that I needed, I knew there was more to it. I sensed it was something of a psychological gesture, more to do with the unconscious than just random reflux of my gut so that my gut told me to go with it if only to find that buried voice deep within my throat that wanted to come out. But I couldn't do it, even after twenty-one sessions of intense probing, simply because I hadn't given myself permission to speak. I had allowed my father to speak for me instead. Consequently, I had given him permission to silence and scare me, so that fear spoke volumes in the burning quiet.

* * *

What about you? Do you see yourself in any of these vignettes?

As we continue, self-awareness via introspection will be the first prescription for you to embrace in your journey of transformation from the inside out. And from introspection comes newfound consciousness, sensitivity, and awareness of your internal emotional workings such as repetitious negative thought patterns that have led you to dysfunctional patterns of behavior, savotaging outcomes for your and your relationships. Introspection *is* a flashlight into the psyche—that which illuminates *what* we do and at times, *why* we do it. Self-awareness is the result.

Unf*cking yourself is predicated on first knowing that you are f*cked up. It's OK; we are all f*cked up to some degree, some of us more than others and with varying coping mechanisms. Knowing that we are is the first step toward changing it. Once our f*cked-up ways are discovered and acknowledged, only then can we begin to transform our lives from the inside out.

Becoming more aware, retraining your mind, and swapping old habits with newer, healthier ones take time. Along the way, as your level of self-awareness increases, I suggest you use what I refer to as your internal "mental stop sign." Put it up as soon as you become aware that the "old ways" are dripping back into your consciousness and stop negative patterns of thinking in their tracks. These negative thoughts will only lead to negative emotions and, ultimately, to negative behaviors. I use this technique personally and professionally. It's basic, concrete, and relatively easy to apply. The only barrier is your mind. Try it. However, be patient with yourself and the technique. Every aspect of change takes time and rehearsal to master.

* * *

CHAPTER 1 WORKSHEET: SELF-AWARENESS AND SELF-CARE

1. What are you most afraid of when you think about change within *yourself?* Describe this fear in detail.

2. What are you most afraid of when you think of change in your *relationships?* Describe this fear in detail.

3. On a scale of 1–10 (1 being least aware and 10 most aware), rate your level of self-awareness. Remember, this only works if you're honest with yourself.

4. Ask your partner or a close friend or family member to rate their perception of your level of self-awareness. Discuss the difference in your self-rating to their rating of your self-awareness level.

5. What are the things you're most aware of that are interfering with progress toward your individual goals?

6. What are the things you're most aware of that are interfering with progress toward your relational goals?

7. What are the things you're least aware of, according to your partner, friends, or family, that are interfering with your relationships?

8. What are the things you're least aware of, according to your partner, friends, or family, that are interfering with your relationships?

9. Do you engage in introspection? If not, why not? How does this make you feel?

10. If you examine all your relationships, past and present, are you aware of any negative patterns you're repeating? If yes, what are they? Where do you think you learned this behavior?

CONGRATULATIONS!

You're on your way to unf*cking your life and relationships from the inside out. Without truly knowing yourself, you cannot truly know others nor join with them in life and love. The journey of purposeful introspection leads to self-awareness, which, in turn, leads to personal growth and development.

UNF*CK THOUGHTS & EMOTIONS:
Projection and Passive-Aggressive Behavior

I HAD A LONG and winding road of self-love yet to tread, around the twists and turns of self-awareness and discovery. Still, I would realize and appreciate that by becoming aware of our projections and passive-aggressive expressions, we can begin to *own our true thoughts and feelings* and, subsequently, *work through them.* I was fortunate to learn and experience this firsthand through my therapy with Dr. Frank. Before delving into projection and passive-aggressive expressions, I would like to be certain that you and I have a shared meaning and understanding of these two concepts and their significance in knowing ourselves, how we relate to others, and how the two are a function of each other.

Let's begin with *projection*. Projection is a self-defense mechanism of unconscious external attribution of unacceptable and uncomfortable internal qualities, impulses, and behaviors to protect the ego. Simply put, it is when psychological information from the inside is misinterpreted as coming from the outside.

Unfortunately, people who project commonly engage in passive-aggressive behaviors—another attempt by the mind to protect the ego from external harm by indirectly expressing negative thoughts and feelings instead of openly sharing and discussing them. Often there is a disconnect between what the person says and does, which can confuse those around them.

Here is an example of projection and passive-aggressive behavior; it is simple yet reflective of complex psychological underpinnings.

Persons A and B are out shopping. Person A turns to Person B and says, "Hey, I think you're hungry; you look hungry to me; we should stop and eat," without any indication from Person B of hunger. Person B replies, "I am not hungry at all; I just ate an hour ago." Despite Person B's response, Person A insists on continuing their observation and experience of Person B's hunger. Person A then says, "Never mind, I am fine and can wait until we get home. I won't starve to death," accompanied by an eye roll and a slight laugh.

Although on the surface, this appears to be a benign inter-action between two people, and, of course, sometimes it can be, repeated similar interactions leave much to be unpacked when trying to understand projections and their residual effects on people and their relationships.

Let's get unpacking!

Person A is not able to identify and take ownership of their hunger, so they project it onto Person B. Person A uncon-sciously misinterprets that which is coming from the inside (them) as coming from the outside; in this case, Person B, despite Person B's insistence that they are not hungry and had already eaten. Why would anyone do that? Simply put, they learned early in life, most likely through their family of origin and other successive relationships, that their needs are unim-portant and should be repressed. However, as illustrated in this example, anytime we are forced to repress our needs, they tend to find an outlet for their expression in forms such as projec-tions—many of which transpire on an unconscious level.

Now that you understand projection, let's identify and unpack the passive-aggressive behavior. It's subtle, but it's there and is often used by passive-aggressive people to disguise their true thoughts and feelings. Person A is not only using passive-aggressive language but also passive-aggressive behavior: "Never mind," "I am fine," "I won't starve to death," the rolling of the eyes, and the laugh. "Never mind" is saying, "my needs are not important to you." "I am fine" means, "I am not fine but scared to tell you how I feel." "I won't starve to death" means "I am starving, but you don't care." The rolling of the eyes shows you that they are annoyed, and the laugh at the end is to wrap up the entire interaction with a bow and bring it back to being a benign exchange between Person B and themselves.

It's akin to when people say, "I am just joking." Often they are not just joking; they are gauging your reaction to their thoughts and feelings. When they sense it will not be well received, they throw in a joking comment to eliminate any possible aggressive undertones. By nature, we are aggressive beings; it's part of our DNA. It's OK! Accept it and learn to manage it so it doesn't interfere with individual and relational functioning.

This begs the next question, a reasonable question I am often asked by my patients: "Well, if I am not conscious of it, then how do I change it?" The short and easy answer is to try to render that which is unconscious into consciousness by working through your past and present patterns of feeling, thinking, and behaving. If you remain unaware, change is unlikely; hence, you will be unable to unf*ck yourself by owning your aggression and projections. (We'll get more into the "how" in Part 2 of this book.)

Only when you're able to own your projections and aggression can you start rejecting what others project on to you, as Person B did in this scene. Rather than accept Person A's projection of hunger, they rejected it. A less self-aware person might have accepted it and responded accordingly. By rejecting others' projections onto you, you will be able to harness your "mental stop sign" and use it when others try to make *their* issues *your* issues. Thus, you learn to manage the problem from the inside out and *not* from the outside in!

As I tell my patients, *stop projecting and start rejecting others' projections onto you*!

Although my projections and passive-aggressive expressions are minimal today compared to how they were before my in-depth work with Dr. Frank, I still feel their emotional tug. Subsequently, I work hard to keep them in their place so they do not interfere with my relationships. Their occupancy in my mind reminds me of their undeniable power and lure to protect myself from harm in my clinical work with others.

IN SESSION WITH DR. FRANK

After thirty sessions, neither my voice nor its permission slip had materialized. My negative semi-unconscious thoughts had a white-knuckle grip on a truth I couldn't face. Seeing my frustration with myself, the mystery of my volition, and knowing I needed a little kick to jump-start my recovery, Dr. Frank had a stroke of genius. He pinpointed the right pressure point to get me to release it out into the open, to myself even.

"The sooner you allow yourself to feel the hurt and disappointment, the sooner you'll progress. So tell me, if only to tell yourself what you need to work through, what we have only touched the surface of!" Although he only raised his voice slightly, gently, for emphasis, all I saw and heard were my father confronting me as if I were stupid.

I had a very real flashback of my father saying, "Damn it, Anita, I order you to talk to me! I'm your father. What's wrong with you?!"

"No!" I yelled. I hushed as my voice broke *sotto voce*. "No."

I could swear my father's ghost was in the room as he replaced Dr. Frank. "Why not? Why can't you face me? Even now? Who am I to you? Who am I? Say it. Say it!"

"Go away."

"No. I'll stay here, facing you, in your face, invading your space until you do. Answer me!"

"I can't. I won't."

"Do it or you're grounded."

"No. That's not fair!"

"Why not?"

"Because I just wanted to feel and be like everyone else. I didn't want to be me. I f*cking hated me."

Then I wept. I sobbed because the truth had gotten out. And I was ashamed and felt guilty for having betrayed my father yet again.

As my father's apparition faded and reality wove back in, I saw Dr. Frank's concerned face. Tears flooded with the treacherous waters of my psyche. I realized I had distorted what he said to me as if I were boiling like the psychological frog in the hot water of my father. I had transferred and projected my negative thoughts and feelings, rooted in my family-of-origin issues and dynamics and my dysfunctional history, onto Dr. Frank and his otherwise neutral comment. I was ashamed because I was a hostage of my negative, repetitive thoughts, conscious and unconscious.

In moments when I feared the past was repeating itself, that fear manifested in transferring a mountain of baggage onto an otherwise innocent comment. It was not so much that all I saw and heard was my father screaming at me, calling me stupid, but that I dreaded and was mortified by the scared-to-death terror that he was only saying something positive to mask what he meant. And that subtext was just as I feared: that my father was, in fact, yelling at me, telling me what to do, with the constant insinuation, as always, that I was stupid and worthless, a prophecy that had been beaten into me until I could not distinguish between prejudice and reality.

Since I couldn't process this conflict or understand the damage that was going on inside me, I projected and transferred it all onto Dr. Frank. But I would soon realize and master this disaster in myself when I came to myself and clinched it in real-time, in reality. I'd learn to stop myself in the act by catching my subconscious thoughts. It was in this experience that I learned about the act of projecting beyond the words in a textbook.

Looking back, I was also trying to reconcile my love and hate for my father. The hate was apparent most of the time. Perhaps *hate* is too strong of a word to describe how I felt. However, it was the only one I had at the time. Despite our very conflicted relationship, oddly enough, I always felt that my father loved me. He just didn't know how to show it or express it since he was stuck in his depression—which presented as anger and irritability most days. With the help of Dr. Frank, I understood it better, and now as a clinician, I can better appreciate my father's mental health challenges. My mother later explained that she believed his depression directly resulted from him leaving his entire family behind to provide a better life and opportunities for his children. He felt lonely and missed his way of life back in India.

After sitting in silence for a good ten minutes, Dr. Frank saw from my reflection that my thoughts had finished dawning, and he chimed in. "Ah, very interesting. You notice even when you address him, you speak to him in the third person. How come?"

"Don't you know, Dr. Frank?"

"I think *you* do."

"OK . . . because I at times feel f*cking paralyzed inside."

We both reflected, and I could see his wheels turning.

"Shall we revisit the thesis incident with Professor Mark Aulls?"

"Well, that's quite the shift, Dr. Frank."

"It's related, as you will learn. Tell me more about it."

I was conflicted about Dr. Frank bringing up Dr. Aulls, who had become my mentor and most revered professor through my graduate studies at McGill University. He was so much more to me than my thesis advisor and supervisor. I looked up to him like a daughter would a father, and I think he knew it and made sure he lived up to that role. We are still friends today.

"I don't want to talk about it, Dr. Frank."

"Anita, you know we need to; you stopped short last time and became very defensive when I mentioned your projections."

Silence. "OK, you're right, you're right. I know I have to work it out. It's just painful."

"I know it is, but that is why you and I are here," he said. "This will help not only personally but professionally. You have to own your projections in order not to project them onto your patients. Don't forget; we are also here for didactic purposes."

"How can I possibly forget that? OK, let's do it then. Let's get it over with. I will continue where I left off last time."

I had entered Dr. Aulls's office in the Department of Educational and Counselling Psychology at McGill University with a poker face hiding the twisted angst of my past, a face I had learned to employ well as I played the part of the straight-A student. I felt like a fraud. I didn't want to reveal that which I feared and bottled up. But as I looked at him, my tears danced on my cheeks and between my unseeing eyes.

Having the 20/20 vision of a man of psyche with acumen into the maladies of the mind, I'm sure Dr. Aulls had already intuited my issues and the theme of my drama. But he simply asked, "What's making you cry?" with compassion in his eyes.

Silence.

Before Dr. Aulls could form his opinion of my work, I had already decided for him that my graduate degree thesis was beyond inadequate. Now, finally, I would be discovered for the fraud I was and would not pass the requirements established by the graduate department at McGill to receive my master's degree. It was this degree I hoped would validate my thoughts and feelings about my intellectual abilities that, indeed, I was not that "stupid little girl" anymore.

Although very much an alpha male, Dr. Aulls was gentle in his approach to my fragile ego. He knew me well enough by now. He calmed me with the balm of his gentle kindness and smile. As I sat and watched anxiously, he flipped through the introduction and stopped.

"Thus far, it looks good, Anita. As you know, it will take some time to go through this, but I will do my best to get it back to you as soon as I can. Stay positive. I am confident that you've done a wonderful job here. After all," he said with a slight smile, "it was written under my direction, and I am certain I directed you well, taught you well, and nurtured your natural talents."

I felt paternally and academically cradled by the comfort of his reassuring words, but despite them, I was certain the draft would prove to him that I was not worthy of his time, attention, and mentorship. I feared he would be upset with me and end our working relationship. I had decided all these things and outcomes based on no concrete evidence, only what I felt and thought, consciously and unconsciously.

"There you have it, Dr. Frank," I said after sharing this experience in our session. "The whole drama with Dr. Aulls and my thesis."

"Thank you, Anita. I know it's hard for you to talk about this, but I know you understand its relevance and importance."

"Of course I do, and thank you for being patient with me."

Tears started to flood with twenty years of pent-up angst and sorrow, with an answer I knew, yet about which I had always been in the dark. I faced my demons once again, the demons that beat me down even in silence, even after they were gone, that terrorized me by looking down on me and made me believe their narratives, even when I desperately wanted to reject them.

* * *

That session with Dr. Frank would prove pivotal in my journey. Although I didn't want to talk about the painful and embarrassing experiences with Dr. Aulls, I knew I had to—for myself and my future patients. It was in this session that my conscious mind awakened to my unconscious, repetitious, distorted, negative projections onto Dr. Aulls. And once awake, I let this cleansing and positive revelation wash over me. I began to accept that perhaps I wasn't that stupid or a fraud, despite my feelings. Dr. Aulls, with the authority of his expertise, had assured me that my work met his standards, even exceeded them—validation I'd never received before. I knew I had to work through my projections, as I learned to call them, that would make it challenging to have a healthy working relationship with Dr. Aulls and every other man who would enter my life and with people in general.

I learned another valuable lesson from this session with Dr. Frank, one I still share with my patients today. Sometimes the best revelations emerge from confronting and working through our conscious and unconscious resistance, as illustrated in the previous session. Initially, I didn't want to talk about it, but Dr. Frank saw through my resistance. Instead of giving in or giving up, he deftly pushed and pulled me through this difficult experience for my growth and development. Often we

> ## Often we don't know what we need until we are in need of it.

don't know what we need until we are in need of it.

I knew that being responsible and holding myself accountable for my thoughts and feelings would help me build healthy relationships from the inside out. I had spent most of my young life walking on eggshells around my father—we all had, including my mother. Everything and anything could easily set him off, ruining the day for everyone. I recall one session in which Dr. Frank helped me to recognize that as innocent as I seemed to be, at times I enjoyed poking the bear.

"You were intentionally picking fights with your father, weren't you?"

"No, OK, yes, I did because he would frustrate me to no end. Not much he did made sense to me, and I guess in hindsight, I was a lot like him in temperament, even though I didn't want to believe it or accept it."

"What happened?"

"Well, I finally confronted him one morning about his f*cking unreasonable behavior and demands. Of course, that did not go well. It never did! I remember being in the kitchen when my father came in all pissed off because his Indian tea wasn't ready. He called out to my mother, 'Where's my chai?

Why aren't you in here making it for me right now?' To which I said, 'Well, why don't you just do it yourself?' He looked at me and replied, 'Why do you do this? You just come here to disturb the shit. I have a system here.' I stood up for my mother, 'Yeah. But it doesn't make any sense. The poor woman is still in bed. You're up. Why can't you just'—he cut in and said, 'You're such a shit-disturber, always questioning everything I do and say. This is between her and me, not you.'"

"Anita," Dr. Frank said, "he did have a point. He was right, but you felt compelled to intervene on your mother's behalf, a role you often played in your family. Yes?"

"Yes. My father was right, and you're right! Perhaps it's the only thing he got right about me. Someone had to stand up for her. I knew she wouldn't stand up for herself. And to be honest, Dr. Frank, I kind of like being a f*cking shit-disturber if it means calling people out on their shit!"

The session continued with a blend of back-and-forth flurries and moments of extended silence. Dr. Frank made me think of how my experiences with him, my father, and my family thus far would impact my development as a future therapist.

"I think you'll find, Anita, that this whole experience will be very fruitful and beneficial for you personally and your career as a psychotherapist. What you learn here for yourself about your ordeals, you'll be able to translate into a working methodology. These insights will help you formulate some very practical and effective theories and techniques for treatment, specific to you, your experiences, and what you learn from our time together."

I listened but felt overwhelmed about the future. I made my way through that session the best way I knew how and committed myself to the difficult, demanding work of contributing to my psychoanalysis. The session ended on that note, and I had much to contemplate before our next session, a session in which Dr. Frank did not take much time to engage after the pleasantries that took place at the beginning of each session.

"I think we're far enough along that we can start confronting the elephant in the room," he said. "Tell me more about your other repetitious, negative behaviors. We touched upon them slightly in previous sessions but not in much depth. You deflect each time I try."

"What do you mean? I think I have already shared a lot with you."

"Barely, Anita. Let us identify clearly, with pinpoint accuracy and surgical precision, your repetitious, negative behaviors. You know, the ones that end the same way, the ones you kind of mention but then quickly skirt away from, the ones that result in the same negative consequences."

We sat in silence—I resented Dr. Frank's accusation of deflection, as I thought and felt I had shared so much and was open and honest about my issues. However, although I did not want to admit it, I knew he was right and probably could see the pain in my eyes at the mention of certain issues originating from my unresolved past and spilling into the present.

"OK, you're right; happy now?"

My analyst looked at me as if to say, *You're finally understanding the true nature of this process, which at times is painful.*

We shared a blank look. But then, sensing the hard climb ahead, I started to weep.

"I f*cking can't do this." I almost got up and left.

But with Dr. Frank's comforting words, I was able to quickly pull myself together as I had always done and remained seated.

"What's making you cry? Put words to these tears."

I choked up again. He handed me a cold bottle of water. I guzzled it, realizing that the nerve-wracking process of being in session had taken more out of me than I had thought. I had learned in class about the emotional challenges of therapy, but experiencing it firsthand in session proved to be a different animal; at times, it felt like more harm than good was being done. Ultimately, I knew therapy would benefit me personally and as a future clinician. How can you help others if you haven't yet helped yourself or experienced sitting on the other side of the couch? One would be at risk of being a *wounded healer*, which would harm patients.

We sat in silence for a few minutes until I felt safe, and the fear and panic subsided.

"Anita, given the state of your relationship with your father, I suspect you seek validation and approval from older men in your life like your expereince with Dr. Aulls. That would be normal, natural, and expected."

I squirmed on the couch.

"Every experience you have shared thus far with older men ends one way: in an apologetic, negative cycle of you feeling inadequate."

"That's not true, Dr. Frank. My relationships are not as f*cked up as you're making them out to be . . . seriously!"

"Aren't they?"

As I mentally put on a sleuth cap and overcoat, shining the psychoanalytic flashlight into my soul, my subconscious, I could reluctantly see the repeating negative pattern to which he was referring.

"Hmm. I didn't think it was that obvious. I'm sorry."

"No need to apologize, Anita, and I am not seeking to be right. Let's just try to understand it further. Do what you did earlier and take control of your process of self-recognition."

As I followed Dr. Frank's instructions, taking control of my process, I struggled with feelings of insecurity and fear. I started to well up with tears, feeling overwhelmed and adrift again, like the world suddenly became charged with darkness. However, I knew Dr. Frank had good intentions. We went on to discuss these patterns in more depth. Dr. Frank was empathic and understanding. I knew that I would have to fight old ways of thinking about myself with new ways. The two clashed in my mind like a thunderstorm. How do you unf*ck the mind after years of f*cked-up internalized experiences? Is it even possible to change such complex internal processes? Clearly, I believed it was, as I had not only committed to the process of change for myself but to a career that was dedicated to and defined by change. But it was difficult given that, at times, I wasn't aware that I was engaging in behavior I was trying to avoid and didn't understand the *why* behind it once confronted by Dr. Frank. Later, Dr. Frank helped me to understand that change was not always predicated on knowing the *why*.

As I put my whole heart and soul into my therapy and my training as a therapist, I began to realize that I was, slowly, changing in ways I had never imagined. The healer in me was emerging. Even my posture and stature were evolving for the better. I was becoming more confident daily as a function of the therapy.

Dr. Frank commented, "Anita, there has been something different about you over the last few sessions. Would you like to share it?"

With a sense of great accomplishment and success, I shared, "Great observation, Dr. Frank; I feel like I am stepping into my destiny." As I basked in my glow as a result of these revelations, I recalled that chai tea incident, in which my dad called me a f*cking "shit-disturber," where the forces of nature and the universe came together to propel me into my destiny as a human being. Since the constellation of my birth, I have been shoehorned between two brothers, always dancing in the middle of their drama and that of my parents. This role of arbiter was thrust upon me so that something about the unavoidability and inevitability of it all, perforce of necessity to survive emotionally, told me the stage was set for who I would be.

Today it's crystal clear I was groomed to dance professionally in the middle of people's conflicts. To help them build healthy relationships from the inside out, I oddly welcome their projections, their passive-aggressive behaviors, and other dysfunctional dynamics with the intention of helping them become more self-aware of what they do, how they do it, and then, of course, to work together to turn it around. In doing so, I am not afraid to use my voice.

"I am pleased for you, Anita. It is your calling."

"Thank you, Dr. Frank, for believing in me and sticking with me through all the mess that is my life. I am trying hard to change and grow from our work together. I know I only see you twice a week. But your voice and our sessions stay with me even when I am not in this room."

* * *

Months later, in therapy as my trust for the process and Dr. Frank grew, I began to feel changes occurring inside of me.

"Change needs to be from the inside out," I revealed. "Self-care and self-love are all a part of it, and I am finally beginning to love myself, Dr. Frank. And you know that's not easy, given the messages I internalized as a child.

"Maybe I am not that stupid after all," I added with a smirk.

"Yes, Anita! I am a witness to your journey of transformation and am happy to be part of it. Maybe you're not stupid? You're *not* stupid. I thought Dr. Aulls's validations and affirmations were helping you. Didn't he recently tell you that you are one of his best graduate students—intelligent, ambitious, industrious? I guess we still have some work to do helping you internalize these thoughts and feelings about yourself."

Upon hearing his name, I became tearful, and my eyes sank. "It's coming to an end soon."

"What is?"

"My time with Dr. Aulls. I feel sad. I am going to miss working with him and just being in his company. He's such a positive force in my life."

"All endings are beginnings in disguise. When the ending ends, it will be a new beginning. You will always have his friendship, and he will always be and serve as your mentor. However, your feelings are valid."

"Honestly? I will feel a little lost now without him. And I am about to start my clinical internship. That frightens me too. Will I be good enough? I don't know. Maybe not! Sometimes that little girl pops back into my head and starts spewing her insecurities. That's so f*cked up. One step forward, two steps back!"

"Despite the progress you've made here, it's normal for some of the negative feelings and narratives you tell yourself to resurface. Sustainable change takes time. You have to keep that 'little girl,' your 'inner child,' in check. As we have discussed in the past, we all have an inner child. That part of us will always be there; hence we need to embrace the child but remember who's in charge. Anita, she is not in charge of your life now. It's the adult you that's in charge."

With each session, I felt a greater trust and faith in Dr. Frank and the therapeutic process. It was an interesting coupling of my therapy and professional training; learning to be a therapist while in therapy was certainly a unique experience.

Weeks later I started the session with, "So I think it's time I talk about the big day."

He looked deep in thought and then asked, "Which one, Anita?"

"The day I literally took off, ran away. That day. The most f*cking defiant day of my life . . . the day that changed my life!"

He looked at me with compassion, intrigued. He knew it was going to be an important session. They all were, but this would be different, and he would have to be on top of his game.

Tears raced down my cheeks before I could even share the story. I guess I had underestimated the emotional weight it still carried in my heart and mind. I cupped my mouth and stared at the door. Then, before I could say anything, Dr. Frank confronted me with what I had not even shared. "Do you want to run away from me as you ran away from your father? It's familiar, isn't it?"

"I do. It is."

"I know you do because that's what you have always done. I am going to ask you to challenge yourself today and stay. I know you are a very determined young woman and appreciate a good challenge."

He handed me a box of tissues. I wiped away my tears.

"Let's continue. Now tell me more about that day, the day you changed your life."

"Well, I was sixteen. One evening, after spending several hours with a group of friends at a local café, we stepped outside to say goodbye before heading off in different directions. Unfortunately, I had missed the last bus and now was stuck for a ride because I didn't have enough money to take a taxi. The notion of walking three miles in freezing temperatures was out of the question. It was getting late, so I asked one of my male friends for a ride. He obliged, and off we went.

"As we rolled up to my house, I glanced up to see my father's car in the driveway. I was terrified. Under normal circumstances, he would not have been home yet; his shift usually ended at 11 p.m. I was deathly afraid and knew what awaited me behind the door. My friend remained in his car to make sure I made it safely inside before driving off. Stopping at my front door, I quickly strategized that I would quietly enter the house, unnoticed (I hoped), and head directly to the sanctuary of my bedroom. I carefully inserted my key and slowly began to turn the knob.

"Suddenly, the door was ripped wide open. My father's familiar glare said all that needed to be said as my mother stood behind him with fear in her eyes. Without saying a word, he grabbed hold of me with foreshadowing violence that made me shudder. It wasn't the first time he had struck me, but something inside told me it would be the last. This time would be different. I knew it in my gut.

"Within seconds, I broke away and ran as I had never run before, without conscious direction or thought. For the first time, my body and mind were in self-preservation mode. At that moment, nothing mattered other than breaking free from him physically and emotionally. I had had enough. As I ran, my friend, who had just dropped me off a few minutes before, pulled up behind me. He took me to his house. I knew then and there that nothing would ever be the same again and things would be totally f*cked up. I didn't know exactly what the future held, but I knew I had to get through the moment and that night."

"Anita, thank you for sharing this with me. What you did takes courage and strength, and you're right: that day changed the trajectory of your life."

"Thank you. My father was right; I disturbed a lot of shit that night and in the days, months, and years to come for my family and me."

"What happened next?"

"I called my mother the next morning. I knew she would be worried. As expected, she begged me to return home. My father interrupted our conversation by grabbing the phone out of her hands and interjected with threats and profanity. He said, 'If you do not return here immediately, you will be disowned by this family.' I immediately hung up, then curled into a ball in bed. What had I done? Did I do this? And what would I do next? How would I survive without money or an education? Would he honestly disown me, his only daughter? All these thoughts and questions circled in my mind like the worst tornado imaginable. I was in shock and had to process my actions. My heart did break for my mother, and I did worry about him taking out his anger on her, but for the first time in my life, I had to, wanted to, take care of my needs. And there and then, my need was to be as far away from him as possible."

"How soon after did you return to get some belongings?"

"The next day, when he was at work. As hard as it was running away from him that night, returning to the house to retrieve my belongings and leaving my mother at the doorstep were harder. She begged me to stay again, but I knew I couldn't. Saying *no* to my mother that day was one of the hardest things I've had to do. I knew I was leaving her behind to deal with him and the mess I had created, and I would no longer be able to protect her or serve as a buffer for them and their unhealthy relationship. I felt a tremendous amount of guilt. I still do today. But I knew I had made the right decision. I could not allow her choices to be my choices. I wanted a different life."

"It wasn't your job to protect her; you were the child."

"Dr. Frank, we have discussed this before; as you pointed out, I was a parentified child. I was born into adulthood, not childhood."

"True."

"Anyway, I never returned home to live after that night. And by the way, he did disown me. I didn't think it was possible, but clearly, it was for him. I think five years went by before we had any communications."

"I am sorry to hear that, Anita. That must have been hurtful."

"Of course it was, Dr. Frank. How would you f*cking feel?"

"I would be devastated. A daughter needs her father."

"I was, and yes, I needed a father. But not one like him. And my search for one continues. Do you know anyone? Am I too old to be adopted?" I joked, to mask my pain.

"Anita, there is much to unpack in those questions and comments. Which one do you want to start with?"

"None of them, not today. Anyway, my father working the second shift allowed me to visit my mother and brothers often. His work schedule was our saving grace."

"Your brothers, you don't talk about them much."

"There is not much to share other than we were close, and they had their challenges with my father, but they were very different to mine. I think in some ways, they had it easier because they were boys, but maybe not. I don't know. I am close to both for different reasons. My older brother and I are only a year apart, and my younger brother is ten years younger. I have always felt more like his mother than his sister. We have had our share of conflict, as siblings do, but overall, we are close. Anyway, I know it wasn't easy on them, either, when I left home. We all suffered in our unique ways. Even though I had left the house, the house never left me."

"What do you mean?"

"Well, I always worried about them and often replayed traumatic scenes in my head. I wasn't over all that shit, Dr. Frank, only away from it. I knew I had f*cked up their lives, too, by doing what I did."

"I understand that and wasn't implying you're *over it*; hence, our work here."

"Sorry. I didn't mean to be rude or talk back."

"No need to be. You weren't rude, and talking back in here is encouraged. Unlike in your home, your voice in this office is central and key."

I looked away from Dr. Frank to avoid the tears on the tips of my lashes. I knew he had struck a chord, as did he. I gathered myself, as I always do, and continued sharing some of the challenges of leaving home as a teen without financial support, a formal education, or anywhere to go. He listened and was very supportive and empathic. I felt like a burden had been lifted, the burden of carrying all those thoughts and emotions for years. Dr. Frank made me feel like my story of leaving home finally had a legitimate voice. His office had become my safe place.

"Oh, yes, before our time runs out, Dr. Frank, I do want to address the comment you made a few weeks ago about my discomfort with Indian people. And yes, it *is* related to what we are talking about, before you accuse me of deflecting."

"I wasn't going to, Anita, but OK, continue."

"It all goes back to how the entire Indian community treated me after I left home, and I am not exaggerating when I say *entire*. They not only shunned me, but some of them shunned my family. It was f*cking horrible. Part of their rancor and utter holier-than-thou disappointment was the perception that I had fallen into the gutter. I was perceived to be worse than the lowest caste in Indian society, worse than an untouchable. Imagine what they thought my future was or what I would be forced to do without a family, Indian values, and the support of a husband in an arranged marriage.

"The negativity, head-tossing, and rolling of eyes I would get when I bumped into them at the mall. It was not so much that I was a cautionary tale, but the perception that I was a rebel who had done this to herself, and deserved all the misfortune coming to me. I had dishonored not just my father, my mother, my family, and myself, but the very way of life Indians hold dear. I had lost everything and deserved it. And to them, I could, henceforth, no longer be saved or redeemed. I was dead to them."

"Anita, that must have been very difficult for you to deal with at such a young age and in addition to everything else. I can't even begin to imagine what that was like, the pain of being rejected by a whole community."

"It was devastating, not only for me but for my family. I f*cking hated them, all of them! I know that sounds terrible, but it's how they made me feel. Anyway, I just avoided them, and even today, I feel very uncomfortable around Indian people. I feel they are judging me. Perhaps I am judging them. I know, I know—I need to own my projections."

"Yes, you do! Not only for your personal growth but for your professional commitment to help everyone irrespective of ethnicity."

"You're right. At least I am aware of it . . . it's the first step."

"Absolutely."

* * *

In the weeks ahead, I shared a great deal more with Dr. Frank about my feelings of rejection from the Indian community and my father. He had rejected me for most of my life, but the rejection I felt after our cut-off was different. It cut more deeply. As I worked on this with Dr. Frank, I realized that I was experiencing him as a father figure, in many ways. He was aware of this and confronted me as any effective therapist should.

"Anita, I know you have been studying this at the institute, and by now know a great deal about the parental feelings that therapy invites, patient toward therapist. In many ways, therapists serve as parental figures to patients. They seek from us the love, acceptance, and nurturance they lacked as children. It's expected over time. Would you like to share your thoughts and feelings about what I have just said?"

"Dr. Frank, why do you have to be so cold and clinical about it? Of course I know all about transference in the therapeutic relationship. Do you think I'm stupid?"

"I don't think that at all—do *you* think that?"

"Why don't you just answer the question, Dr. Frank, and stop hiding behind your f*cking theoretical concepts!?"

"I did answer your question, but clearly it wasn't good enough. You're angry with me."

"No shit. After all this time with you. I don't know what I was thinking. You don't care about me either. This is all psychobabble bullshit! Why would I ever think you cared about me?"

I sat in awkward silence for a while. I was embarrassed and ashamed of my outburst. He was right. I was projecting onto him my feelings of being stupid and that he was not caring. I thought I had learned to stop doing this. Clearly, I had not and still needed to work on myself.

Dr. Frank broke the silence. "Anita, let me be clear—I don't think you're stupid, and I do care about you and your progress. I think you have a bright future ahead of you personally and professionally. Please, let's work through these thoughts and feelings. I know you're feeling vulnerable right now, and that's OK. I am here for you."

The little attempt at levity with his gentle, kind demeanor touched me.

"Your heart is showing," I said.

"Good, then you're seeing me more clearly. I am not a technician, Anita. I am human like you. And as you're learning and experiencing, therapy is a very intimate and complex process."

"Yes, I can see that and feel it, too, Dr. Frank." I wiped the tears from my face and put myself back together again, as I had many times before, not just in therapy but in life.

"I only have unconditional, positive regard for you, and it's a privilege to be a part of your growth and development as a therapist in training. You misapprehend because, at times, you do not hear my voice. You only hear your voice and your father's voice. Furthermore, you hear your father's voice in your interactions with other older men. Subsequently, your reaction to them is based on the primary imprint left in your mind and heart from the negative interactions with your father. The mind can't help but recreate and replay old scenarios because there is a strong unconscious desire to resolve them, make peace with them, through the new people in your life who resemble them."

I knew he was right. "I'm sorry. I'm trying. I am, but I'm afraid."

"You're only afraid because you've given your father's

voice and the voice of the past subconscious permission to let you be afraid."

And on that note, our session came to an end. I was left with much to think about as I continued on this path of self-discovery, incising with even more surgical precision than ever before.

* * *

As I reflected on our session, it became clearer that when irrational feelings that originate in past experiences sneak their way into current interpersonal spaces, they must be confronted and resolved to the best of our abilities. We must work through them in real time. By doing so, we minimize the risk of the past repeating itself in our minds and in our relationships.

* * *

Unlike most sessions in which Dr. Frank waited for me to start, one day, he was particularly assertive and took the lead.

"Anita, I have been thinking about our work thus far and want you to know that I think you're making great progress. I know at times our sessions are difficult. That's expected because, as you know personally and as a student in training of this craft, things we avoid outside these walls are the things we give life to in here. I know you have felt vulnerable in some of your disclosures, and vulnerability is not something you do well. But you're getting better and better at letting your walls down with each session. Our walls—defense mechanisms such as our projections—are there to protect us; most of the time, they serve us well. However, sometimes they stand in the way of our emotional and psychological progress. One brick at a time, we will reduce their ability to do that to you in your life. Through our work together, you will eventually have access to and enter the most profound heights of your psyche, as you unlock a power within you to help others do what you're doing here with me."

"Wow, Dr. Frank, that's quite an opening statement. Thank you for that, and yes, I sometimes wonder if any of this is helping me. Some sessions I do feel like quitting, but I persevere because I believe in the process. How can I not? I am committing to this profession, to the seat you're sitting in today. I appreciate your words."

"You're welcome, Anita! The goal is to be an integrated self, a self that incorporates the good, the bad, the feared, the complicated, the unresolved, and so on. Do you still feel like running away?"

I nodded, ramping up the magnification by a factor of ten.

"Isn't it interesting that by separating from your father, by running away literally from him, you ran into him more intimately? You began to see from his eyes when you saw for yourself what it was like to try and survive in the world with very little support and resources. In a sense, by running away, you ran not so much straight back to his embrace but into the very heart of who he was and why he was, didn't you?"

I allowed myself to take this all in.

"Then I guess I can't run away from the past or my father?" I said, in self-analysis.

"How come?"

"Probably for the same reason you can't run away from yourself, Anita. Because from birth, your parents, especially your father, become intimate programmers of your software and hardware, of your mental code, and as such, they become not just a part of you but second nature. You don't know when, what, or why they influence you to do or say a certain thing at any given time."

"It's a powerful contradiction, isn't it?" he said. "Sometimes, as we drive on the road of life, we are driven by our demons, ghosts, internalized shadows, personas that become like a bank account of our information, from which we respond to others, ourselves, to situations, and, thus, to life itself."

"Yes, isn't it, though, Dr. Frank? If that's the case, then the mind is the vehicle for the heart and soul. I think you've hit upon a good metaphor. It might be just me, foolishly trying to find logic in the four chambers of the human heart, but why do I sense there's some logic to be mined and excavated from the subconscious, like a negative-unconscious archeological dig site? I don't know if I'm making any sense."

"Yes, you're right, Anita. And it makes perfect sense. But *why*, do you think?"

"Hmm. Well, since the mind is the vehicle for the soul and heart, and intelligence the road on which it travels, then it's only logical that to be unconsciously or mindlessly driven by a subconscious we are not aware of and, therefore, not in control of, is not just undesirable but leads into tight spots, dead ends, negative and tragic situations that cry out for professional help from someone like me. I suppose I'll understand that with full-circle sense when I'm on the other end of the therapist's couch. Thus, it follows, like a nonsensical and yet very reasonable sequitur, that if no one is at the wheel, the vehicle will wander, constantly crashing into life's circumstances, until the road of life ends or the mental car is put out of commission. Either way, this inevitably leads to rendering the conveyance and automobile of life—the body, mind, heart, and soul—out of service when a final and absolute collision requires either a mental mechanic to tune things up or a coffin. Hmm. What do you think we can deduce from that as psychotherapists?"

"Well," he said, "what do *you* deduce?"

"Dr. Frank, I can only conclude that since understanding our character, feelings, motives, beliefs, narratives, and desires is a substantial factor in the burgeoning of general inferential processes and general intelligence, it's rather conspicuously clear that the ability to get in the driver's seat in life involves the capability to self-organize. This is necessary to execute a course of action and drive on that old and winding road of love and relationships, especially because getting behind the wheel of that family Buick sets us up for self-efficacy. And that is a function of self-awareness, self-driving, self-governance, and self-control and, thus, readies us, most importantly, for success to manage our direction, to get where we want to go in life and love versus being driven by the rain inside the streets of our souls."

"Very true, Anita; so, in other words . . . ?"

"So in other words, self-steering navigation and, thus, self-efficacy, allows us to avoid the pitfalls on the road of life and love, the obstacles created by negative, unconscious repetition that cause flat tires and damage to the apparatus and machinery that is us. In this new approach, the sufferer will not just be undeterred by setbacks, she'll avoid most setbacks altogether. Suddenly self-enlightened, this person will be self-aware of her vices, flaws, and abilities. She'll be able to apply these abilities with new eyes and a new game plan as she course-corrects on a new love map in the relationship universe she never knew existed. Before, she was unaware of these negative reactions and repetitions and, thus, was unable to change her attitudes or her thought-and-relationship patterns. Indeed, how can she change and get to something she didn't even know existed?"

"Well said."

"I didn't quite connect the dots before this session, Dr. Frank, or didn't so eloquently, I mean. But I see now how strong self-awareness equals strong self-efficacy, which equals a good grip on the rainy streets of life and smooth driving on the road of existence, ensuring fewer accidents and fewer obstacles. In this way, you can get where you want to go in life and relationships."

We shared a warm, tacit understanding.

* * *

This was all definitely leading somewhere, but the real turning point in my journey of self-awareness happened on another stormy night when I was studying in the library. I had been burning the candle at both ends. In a time crunch, I panicked when my next session with Dr. Frank snuck up on me, and I was forced to choose between my exam grade and passing the test of my journey into the psyche. I choked and decided to short-change the currency of positive change for the sake of my GPA.

But as I tried to cancel my session with Dr. Frank, I ran into the full-metal wall of reality when he, now disappointed in me, or maybe I was projecting and I was just disappointed in myself for letting him down, said he'd have to charge me extra. As a student who struggled financially and worked numerous jobs to make ends meet, I just could not afford to do that. So I took an authoritative tone.

"You should be understanding. You're my therapist," I said. Telltale lightning struck outside the library window as I continued to thunder at him.

But he just said, detached, "No, you obviously don't respect or value the process. We've been at this for some time now, and you know my policy and agreed to it in our first sessions, so this should not come as a surprise to you, frankly."

"Dr. Frank, it's clear that all you care about is the fee-for-service and could give a shit about me. Seriously, you're just like my father, never there to help me when I needed it. Again, pointing out my inadequacies and all that I am doing wrong. I thought, of all the people in the world, you would understand."

"It's not that at all. As a student of the profession, you know that the fee has nothing to do with my reaction to you canceling the session at the last minute. In fact, the last few times you did this, I didn't charge you nor comment on it. But now that it has happened again, I have no choice but to question your commitment to the process and respect for my time and our work. And I think in some ways, it's you running away from me as you did from your father. You're afraid somehow that I will hurt you as he hurt you, and you'll discover that I am not trustworthy after all. You will reject me before I reject you."

"Dr. Frank, don't you think that's overanalyzing a simple cancelation?"

"Anita, I think you know exactly what I am referring to. A cancelation here and there within a reasonable amount of time is expected, but the pattern in which you have been canceling sessions, coupled with what we have been talking about in sessions, forces me to confront you. Any good therapist would fail their profession if they did not address this, as I am doing right now. Please reflect on this, and I will see you next week."

After hanging up with him and thinking through his comments about commitment, respect, running away, and my fear of rejection, I realized he was right. Although I appeared to be all-in, I realized I had been holding back somewhat, especially after the session in which he talked about my difficulty with being vulnerable and rejection. I was projecting my fears onto him rather than confronting them as he had just done on the phone. Although I was still upset with his rigidity about the fee, I understood and respected his rationale. I once again learned that as much as we say we want to change as humans, a part of us resists the process in a desperate effort to protect ourselves from the unknown.

After that incident, my commitment to the therapeutic process and Dr. Frank turned a symbolic and much-needed corner. My awareness heightened that I had a lot more work to do from the inside out. From that day forward, I never violated his cancelation policy out of respect for him, the process, and my growth and development. I recognized that I had so much more work to do emotionally toward owning my projections and other yet-undiscovered unconscious negative thoughts and feelings. I was a work in progress and was grateful to be working with someone who called me out for my emotional bullshit.

Today I share this story with my clients when they're faced with a similar situation. Dr. Frank was correct in his approach, assessment, and confrontation, and I appreciated him as an authority when he needed to be. For the first time I was able to accept and embrace his authority differently than I had with my father.

With this revelation, I could see my father look at me from long distances, from the past. Then I saw the light dawning. It was my new glow of self-awareness, which included dancing differently with my projections and, for the first time, rejecting his projections onto me, and anyone else's for that matter.

For the first time, I had muted him, my father. Then I knew I was on to something life-changing, something beautiful and transformative. Like when I first fell in love with the image and possibility of becoming a healer. I was going to be a therapist and be proud of helping people. It would be my passion, my vocation, and my life's purpose. My transformation was underway, compliments of the process of self-awareness via introspection and the complete cessation or minimization of projections. The path of least resistance, projection, and transference was the easy way out compared to some of the complicated dynamics Dr. Frank was helping me unf*ck about myself and my relationships.

As a woman of fortitude, I was never one for the most facile way if I could help it. It was simply a revelation to be relished, that I could re-contextualize my conflict and issues with my father in terms of the enlightened how-to of a therapist in training. Now with open eyes and intellect, I was no longer a pawn at the mercy of forces beyond my control. I said to him and for him everything he couldn't say himself, such as the loving intent behind his treatment of me, as I realized he wanted the best for me as most parents want for their children. However, he, like many, was stuck in the quandary of having to survive in the world.

It brought me great satisfaction to begin the journey of conquering my issues en route to mastering them as much as anyone can. I knew I was starting to take control of thoughts, feelings, and actions that had once hijacked my mind, body, soul, and heart. I recognized selflessly my father's troubles, which manifested as a result of his endeavor to survive by his wits and industry in a very challenging world. Presently, I could detach myself from my once-unresolved issues that I inherited from my father. Still, I also saw that this inheritance contained positive, advantageous, and empowering qualities such as self-reliance and an unquestionably excellent work ethic. In the end, his gift was intelligence that resulted from my being thrown into confusion so early on—order from chaos. His gift was my unique perspective, and, whereas he never resolved his issues nor was he aware of them, I had the privilege of therapy, a privilege he never had.

* * *

This was my inside-out journey of unf*cking my life and my relationships. Now it's your turn to look within, to increase your self-awareness and knowledge about your projections, reject others' projections onto you, and work through passive-aggressive behaviors. In the following worksheet, you'll encounter discriminating questions that can help you start distinguishing those damaging patterns from the white noise of the psyche, which will, over time, allow you to replace them.

Let's keep going!

* * *

CHAPTER 2 WORKSHEET: PROJECTION AND PASSIVE-AGGRESSIVE BEHAVIOR

1. Identify thoughts and feelings that make you feel uncomfortable.

2. Identify any thoughts and feelings that are difficult for you to share with others.

3. How were these thoughts and feelings dealt with in your family of origin?

4. How were these thoughts and feelings dealt with in your past and/or current relationships?

5. Reflect on your past/current relationships; are you repeating certain negative patterns of interaction? If so, which ones and how?

6. Practice expressing thoughts and feelings that are difficult in a daily journal. At the end of a week, write a summary of the thoughts and feelings you recorded and how it felt to identify and acknowledge them.

7. Verbally share your thoughts and feelings with your partner or a close friend/family member. *Verbal communication is impactful in a different way, and the practice of it will make it easier for you to continue to engage in this type of conversation.*

8. You can only start rejecting other people's projections once you know where your issues start and stop. What have you started to reject?

9. How does it *feel* to *reject* others' projections?

10. How do you know they are not your projections? Remember, projections are thoughts, feelings, and actions that are misinterpreted as coming from the outside when, in essence, they are coming from the inside. Provide an example.

11. Have you been repeatedly accused of being passive-aggressive? If so, identify one or more of those passive-aggressive behaviors and record it.

12. Do you repeatedly agree to do things but then secretly resent doing them?

13. Do you repeatedly not follow through on things that you have agreed to do?

CONGRATULATIONS!

You're on your way to unf*cking your
life and relationships from the inside
out by taking ownership of your
thoughts and feelings and rejecting
others' projections. As your journey
unfolds and you start to change, others
around you will be perturbed.
They will adapt and adjust with you
or be left behind.

PART 2
Working Together

UNF*CK TALKING:
Verbal Communication

IF REMEMBRANCE IS a painter, then my colorful story is about to paint a masterpiece of a portrait of how dysfunction by self-awareness can bring about clear communication from miscommunication, from stuck silence to eloquent healing. This is how you can find or rediscover your voice—by learning, or rather relearning, what it is to be human. Get "back to the basics" of life and love to effectively attend to the universal human need and desire to intimately connect with others—*intimately* being the operative word and biggest challenge in an era ruled by less intimate communication. Although social media and various forms of electronic communication may *feel* intimate, they are far from forging the emotional intimacy we crave and need.

I believe we risk becoming emotionally illiterate as our conversational skills decrease and our use of electronic forms of communication increases. Yes, we are communicating more as a society; however, I would argue that the quality of those communications is poor and has a net negative impact on our relationships.

I frequently hear stories in my practice such as: "I don't feel connected to my partner anymore, and I don't know why. We never have a conversation. Although we text each other often throughout the day, it's always about random, superficial shit. It's like we just don't know how to talk to each other anymore . . . it's so sad."

Sound familiar? If so, you're not alone.

Based on my clinical experience, this is becoming an increasing problem during the birth and rise of e-communications. Our communications tend to be less grounded in building emotional intimacy. I assert that true emotional intimacy with another cannot be built, developed, nurtured, or maintained without engaging in face-to-face dialogue, rich in emotional and physical cues that enhance the communicative experience. E-communications have a time, place, and purpose, but they should not be substitutes or replacements for verbal conversation. Talking together is one of the essential things in life and love you need to return to to unf*ck your life and your relationships; it needs to be coveted and protected.

In the following pages, I will help you unf*ck your communication skills by guiding you back to the basics of "active listening" and "effective speaking" in addition to helping you explore and understand some of your f*cked-up ways of communicating that trace back to your family of origin. As a child, I internalized faulty and destructive modes of communication. As I have shared, I grew up with a father who mostly yelled and told me not to speak unless I was spoken to. And for years, I didn't speak—until I found my voice and the courage, strength, and desire to use it.

Following is a brief story to illustrate how communication struggles interfered with my relationships and, in turn, how those struggles made me feel about myself.

IN SESSION WITH DR. FRANK

"I was around seventeen years of age, and I had been invited to meet my boyfriend's parents for the first time," I told Dr. Frank as he took notes.

"How did it go?"

"As far as I could tell, the dinner ended without incident, and I thought it had gone well. But after talking to Oliver the next morning, I realized maybe it hadn't gone well at all; his parents apparently liked me but asked if I spoke. Am I that f*cked up?"

"Anita, you're not f*cked up."

We sat in silence for some time. I was clearly perturbed by the discrepancy in the experience of that night. Sharing it with Dr. Frank made it seem more real. I guess the silence lasted even too long for Dr. Frank, who didn't want me to leave the session without discussing my feelings.

"How did that revelation make you feel?" he asked.

"To be honest, initially, I was offended and hurt by this feedback. Later, however, through much self-reflection and awareness, I realized that I had been instructed not to speak since birth. I recall my father saying, 'Just listen, don't talk; you might say something stupid and embarrass me.' Until that evening with Oliver's family, I did not fully grasp the magnitude of the internalization of this message and its impact on my self-esteem, confidence, and ability to interact with others or that it was my overall 'internal blueprint for communication.' Those who know me well today cannot imagine a time in which I rarely spoke."

"Conclusions?"

"We don't have to be our past. Blueprints drawn in child-hood through our interactions with our parents can be redrawn and reshaped. My father trained me well to engage in shouting matches, shutting up, and listening, but not so well in engaging in conversations and resolving any issues—ever! The lyrics by Cat Stevens in his famous song 'Father and Son' describe my life at home best: 'From the moment I could talk I was ordered to listen.' Makes me tear up every time! Once I left home, though, I quickly learned that this would not work in the outside world. I am learning to change my ways from the inside out. I obviously still have more work to do. Don't we always? Isn't that why I am here with you?"

"Yes, it is. Early-childhood exposure to unhealthy communication patterns resulting in other issues such as low self-worth and confidence, to name a few, can be resolved. You're living proof of it."

"Thank you, Dr. Frank." And on that note, our session came to an end.

As illustrated in this vignette, although this foundation in "listening" equipped me well for my profession, it took years to master my effective communication skills personally and professionally. Swapping my old internal blueprint for a new one helped me find my voice and use it with intention, purpose, power, and strength and to help others do the same.

ELECTRONIC COMMUNICATION

Although I struggled with every aspect of effective communication in my youth, I feel fortunate that at least I didn't have to deal with the added complexities of social media and other forms of electronic communications as people do today. While advancements in electronic communications via email, FaceTime, Zoom, texting, and social media platforms have seemingly made aspects of our lives easier, they have made other aspects more complicated, difficult, and even harmful.

The value and need for electronic communication was greatly demonstrated during the COVID-19 pandemic when these mediums served as lifelines for many people. Families and friends could stay connected virtually, and some people could return to work, although in a very different way. For myself, I was able to continue my work through Zoom. Although it was much different from being in person, it was better than the alternative of interrupting therapy or possibly ending therapy altogether during a period when mental health services were most needed.

Without such technology, the pandemic's impact on our mental health would have been worse. It's amazing in an ironic sense; however, a reliance on remote interaction is not without negative consequences on our minds and our relationships. The very thing it was intended to improve—communication and our sense of global connectedness—is the very thing that is being impacted negatively. Yes, we are communicating more, but the quality of these communications is causing our relationships to suffer. We unintentionally have traded frequency and expediency for depth and quality.

SOCIAL MEDIA

Although it is beyond the scope of this book to address the plethora of the emerging research on the impact of social media on our lives, it does need mentioning because of its impact on our psyches and relational world. At this point, research findings conclude the following ten statements:

1. It is designed to be addictive; its use reinforces the reward center of the brain by releasing dopamine, the feel-good hormone.

2. Using it frequently, which most do because of its addictive nature, is associated with an increase in depression and anxiety.

3. It provides a distorted lens of people's lives and personal appearances.

4. It takes away from "in the moment" experiences.

5. It increases opportunities for harmful interactions, especially among younger people, such as cyberbullying.

6. It reinforces our infantile need for immediate gratification.

7. The frequency and intensity of its use keep people from having real-life experiences in their community.

8. It encourages unhealthy comparisons to others (physical, financial, lifestyle).

9. It fosters FOMO: fear of missing out.

10. It causes us to lose productive time. People sometimes spend hours a day swiping left and right when they could be engaged in real-life satisfying activities with concrete results.

* * *

These findings are alarming and should concern us. However, I believe with proper guidance and established rules, we can learn to use social media to our benefit, not our personal and relational demise. *Prescriptions to manage these challenges are outlined in the following pages.*

Professionally, I can attest to the preceding data. People regularly seek my services to deal with their anxiety or stress brought on by social media engagement. I have heard stories of being dumped by a change of "status" on Facebook, being excluded from parties as evidenced by certain persons' posts, misperceived intent behind a comment or a picture, and so on.

This is reoccurring enough in my clinical work that I coined the term "social media distress disorder" (SMDD) to conceptualize the problem better. SMDD refers to all emotional and physical distress caused by some type of social media experience.

My experience on social media has not been that different from that shared by my patients and friends. Consequently, I only engage in social media for career purposes: to promote my message, mission, and passion for bringing awareness to mental health issues and helping others to unf*ck their life and relationships.

Even in that limited capacity, I use social media platforms with specific self-monitoring rules, which work well and keep my mental health in check and my relationships aligned. These rules help increase my positive experience on social media, decrease negative consequences, and adjust any imbalance in the right direction. As a result, I am able to focus more on real-life activities and experiences and less on social media. I encourage you to do the same.

Here are some suggestions to help you minimize experiencing SMDD, all of which are predicated on your commitment to "self-monitor." For the purpose of our work, I define self-monitoring as the ability to track and regulate thoughts, feelings, and behaviors around a defined task, in this case, social media platform engagement. And to ensure this, I suggest keeping a log.

Time. Identify and understand your current usage patterns. How much time do you spend on a given day on social media? Use a timer and log the results or just check your phone; it will tell you. How does your actual usage time compare with your perceived usage time? Often there is a large discrepancy between the two, and people are shocked by the reality of wasted hours. Use this confrontation to allocate more time to *real-life, in-person* activities in your community with friends, family, or alone. And with this reality, establish new rules around usage: how much time is appropriate and at which times it's appropriate. I recommend the following: never at mealtimes unless it's to take a picture (of people, not just your food), never in place of a real-life experience, never interfering with an important scheduled event, and usage time needs to be discussed with your partner. This last item is most important. If your partner often remarks that you're "always on your phone," then you probably are and need to start making changes.

Place. Identify *where* you use social media/phone the most. Unfortunately, many people use it in the most inappropriate places—dinnertime, social settings, work, while driving (dangerous), and while walking, to name a few. I suggest putting the phone away when you're in a social setting with others. No one likes it when someone pulls out a phone in the middle of a conversation. If it's not an emergency and not for photographic purposes, place the phone where it isn't visible. Be present and fully engaged in the moment.

Purpose. Ask yourself what purpose your post, comment, or picture will serve. Sometimes we are unaware of it, but I believe most of what we share is purposeful and intentional although at times unconsciously driven. Unfortunately, the intention is not always positive. I encourage you to use social media to inspire, appreciate, motivate, and educate. The next time you're getting ready to share something on a platform, ask yourself, "Am I adding to the toxicity or the positivity on social media?"

Log off. Instead of only closing or minimizing a social media site or app, sign off completely between use. This creates another layer between you and the platform. You might use it less if you have to enter your username and password each time. I suggest this to my patients often, and they almost always report that it does help them spend less time on social media. Try it!

Don't post after a breakup. Post-breakup is an emotional time, and the last thing you need to do is share your drama with the world. Social media platforms should not be used as your "therapist." Resist the urge to post about your feelings, your ex, or your new relationship. Instead, call a friend or make an appointment with a real therapist.

Schedule a detox day. Take one day out of the week to stay logged off. Give your body and mind a break from technology. You might be surprised at how free and refreshed you feel.

Pause before posting. Reexamine your drafted post one last time before you decide to share it with the world. And be *sure* that's what you want the world to know about you. Once it's seen or read, it can't be unseen or unread. Yes, you can delete it, but someone, somewhere may have captured a screenshot. So be thoughtful and mindful before pulling the trigger.

Check yourself. The worst time to post on social media is when you're having a bad day. Instead of taking those emotions and thoughts to the world, take them to a friend or family member, go for a walk, engage in an activity to help you reframe your mindset, or call your therapist.

Be inspired rather than compare. Instead of comparing yourself to other people's lifestyles and appearances—some of which only represent glossy highlights and not the reality of their lives—let the genuine success stories inspire you to improve your life. Being a fitness person, I am always inspired by other fitness buffs who are doing better than myself. Their posts, comments, and pictures motivate me to work harder.

Get back to real life. Recognize that social media is not a replacement for face-to-face activities and interactions. Social media does not and should not take away from real-life experiences with real people. If you find yourself spending more time with your virtual friends than real friends, it's time to make a shift. Join a gym or social club, pick up a hobby—anything to venture out into the real world, stepping away from your virtual persona.

TEXTING

I appreciate the simplicity, efficiency, speed, and immediacy of technology's ability to exchange data via e-communication, especially texting. But it is the most inefficient and arguably a more problematic way to communicate about conflict and personal issues.

In my professional and personal experience, texting often leads to greater misinterpretations and misunderstandings (unless it's strict data exchange, such as pick-up and drop-off times, quick reminders, or cancellations). Written words don't accurately convey tone, emotions, facial expressions, gestures, body language, and eye contact. Words themselves seem less meaningful when they deny us the human experience of hearing the sound of the other's voice, seeing their gestures, and tuning in to other physical/social cues that reinforce that, indeed, we are engaged in the conversation.

Also, people are much less likely to have meaningful conversations through texts and engage in passive-aggressive behavior, often saying brash and brazen things to one another that they would not share in person. "Cowards behind keyboards" is a term I often hear from my clients to describe such behavior.

The real message is often lost through the medium; the medium is part of the problem. Conversations are fragmented and reduced to words and pictures. Intonations and facial cues are absent, hiding people's emotions, resulting in further miscommunications in deciphering the message's intention. Interpretations are also subjective; my mindset, mood, and the pace I bring to reading a text will determine my understanding of it. If it lacks crystal clarity, what I receive may be very different from the sender's original intent. We project our emotions onto these words that come to us emotionless. In that process, so much is lost in translation and even distorted.

I have listened to a plethora of stories from patients who have had to send multiple text messages to correct a misunderstanding orginating from one message. I have encouraged them (as I do you) to merely pick up the phone and have a verbal conversation to avoid further relational complications and misunderstandings, and to stop the flurry of messages going back and forth. These continuous text exchanges in adults lead to various individual emotional problems and relational breakdowns. And for teens, such threads can impede their interpersonal development (not to mention affect their ability to use proper grammar, spelling, and punctuation!).

I am not suggesting we eliminate technology from our lives because frankly, that would be impossible and unrealistic. However, I am advocating that we learn to use it with certain guidelines and pay close attention to time, place, purpose, and the other forms of self-regulation, as noted. Use technology to make life simpler, not more complicated by creating miscommunication and unintended consequences that cause relationship problems.

To avoid emotional collateral damage via text, apply these basic rules:

1. **Do not write a novel nor respond in novel form.** If you need a lengthy message to communicate your thoughts and feelings, arrange for a time and day to speak with each other instead of texting. Conversely, if someone sends you a novel, tell them you would prefer to speak with them instead. Or bypass the step of arranging for a time and just pick up the phone and call them. I know responding to a text via a phone call is considered a faux pas, but better that than risking miscommunication. If the call is not taken and they reply with a text such as, "What's up," text back and arrange for a time and place to talk.

2. **Don't ghost someone.** Ghosting, as we know, refers to not responding to someone at all; it is very rude and dismissive. According to my patients, this is a normal occurrence in the dating world. Don't be that person. Instead, respond to their message respectfully. For example, if you've gone on a date and lacked chemistry, but they were interested and continued to text, just respond with a generic, "It was great to meet you, thank you for a lovely night, and good luck with your future dates." This type of message avoids hurting the other person but lets them know that you're not interested in pursuing the relationship further.

3. **Sexting should be between consenting adults (if ever).** Don't do it unless you know 100 percent who's on the receiving end.

4. **Do not use ALL CAPS.** If you feel the need to scream to communicate your thoughts and feelings, you know it will not end well. Instead, pick up the phone and call them or arrange a face-to-face conversation.

5. **Do not use texting to resolve conflict or to confront.** Nothing good can happen. Using texting for this purpose often leads to miscommunication, misinterpretation, and other unintended consequences. Pick a location, establish a time (good information to exchange via text), and then have an in-person, verbal conversation about the problem. Just talk about it!

6. ***Do* show signs of love.** Send a friendly emoji.

7. ***Do* use text for data exchange.** Texting is best for confirmations, cancelations, verifying an address, and so on. All things factual that can't be misinterpreted. For example, "I will pick you up at 10 a.m." is a perfect use of this technology.

8. **Don't break up with someone over a text.** Be mindful and thoughtful of the other person's feelings. Have some respect for yourself and the other person by at least calling them on the phone if you're not meeting in person. No one likes to be dumped in a text or on social media.

* * *

These are simple strategies to help you get back to the basics of love and life by talking to one another, and use technology at the appropriate time, place, and purpose to unf*ck your life and relationships, not to f*ck them up further. Let it be a means to simplify communication and not further complicate it.

EFFECTIVE VERBAL COMMUNICATION

Everything starts with a conversation, and a conversation is not a text exchange or an experience over social media. It is a face-to-face, verbal dialogue between people. I believe it is the most effective way to resolve relational challenges. Relationships f*ck us up, and the only way to get unf*cked is to sit down and talk to each other. It's simple, it's basic, and yet it's so difficult for many to do! A verbal conversation can never be replaced by written words or skipped if we hope to build emotional intimacy and resolve problems. Sharing words is the vehicle through which we make contact and move from problems to solutions. When I prescribe "the talking cure," as Freud called it, to my patients, the following common scenario takes place:

"That's it? That's all you have to say, Anita—talk to her?"

"For now, yes."

"Well, that's pretty basic. Is this a trick or something?"

"Are you able to talk to her about it?"

"No. Mostly I try to avoid her and the topic because I am tired of it. Can't you give me some strategies or something? We text each other more than we talk. It's easier."

"Of course it's easier. You don't have to look at her and can hide behind the written words. I can, and of course, I will give you strategies. But first, I will help you improve your communication skills so you can use the strategies I share with you. Nothing can be accomplished without a verbal conversation about the challenges you're experiencing, from your perspective and hers. Texting is not the same as sitting down with her to talk. So much is lost in that form of communication."

"OK, you're right. It's easier to text because I can avoid having the real conversation that I am afraid to have. I make myself feel better by telling myself that I tried, when I haven't. And you're right, she often just wants to talk, and I have a million excuses not to."

"We need to learn to walk before we can run."

UNF*CK TALKING

* * *

There are so many aspects of communication. Where do we start? My years of personal psychoanalysis, formal academic training, and over twenty-five years of clinical experience with individuals, couples, and families inform and guide my belief that we need to master basic verbal communication skills before attempting to solve individual or relational problems. Routinely, I help people master "effective talking" and "active listening." Do you notice the use of the terms *active* and *effective*? I believe mastering these two skills will go a long way toward unf*cking your life and your relationships. Most of us are born with the ability to do both; however, how we employ these basic communication skills is determined largely by our family-of-origin dynamics and our subsequent relational experiences. Over the years, your pattern of communication, like so many other behaviors, is either encouraged or discouraged via positive and negative reinforcements. And, of course, the advent of e-communications has weakened these skills, as we've already discussed. Once you learn to communicate effectively, you can begin tackling any relationship challenges. Any successful conversation is one in which active listening and effective talking occur in tandem.

ACTIVE LISTENING VS. PASSIVE LISTENING

When we think of activities, we generally don't place listening in that category. Most likely this is because, as in any activity, our success depends on whether we are passive or active in our required role. Unfortunately, I believe most of us are "passive listeners." To become effective communicators, we first must accept and understand that we are always communicating in one form or another. Everything we do or don't do, verbally and nonverbally, conveys a message. Passive listening communicates overall negativity, while active listening communicates positivity. How are the two different? Passive listening is a mechanical, one-way process in which the listener doesn't provide any cues or gestures to assure they are paying attention or care about what the speaker is trying to communicate. They hear the words and sounds but fail to attend to them or engage in an expected manner:

"Sorry, what did you just say?"

"Never mind, I am done with this conversation. I don't know where you are, but you're definitely not here in this conversation."

That's a perfect vignette to illustrate the dynamics between a passive listener and the speaker.

Solutions can never be arrived at when you're stuck in a conversation with a passive listener. In observing interactions between people in my office and in my personal life, it's clear that many people engage in passive listening—a problem I believe is exacerbated and rising due to the amount of time and attention spent attending to our smartphones.

Active listening, on the other hand, is two-way communication, or sometimes more, in which the listener fully engages in the conversation through physical gestures and verbal responses. They might lean in or out depending on cues given by the speaker. At times they interject appropriately with questions or comments to illustrate that they are trying to understand the intended message. They are in sync and in tune with the speaker. It's a healthy back-and-forth dance of communication in which the information shared is being attended to and leads to further conversation rather than a shutdown.

We are all guilty of engaging in passive listening at times. Yet we know it is not an effective listening practice in our intimate relationships, especially when trying to resolve issues. We need to be able to actively listen to unf*ck our life and relationships. Here are some ways you can become a more effective, active listener:

1. **Stop talking.** This seems obvious, but it's not so simple. Most people like the sound of their voice and are focused on themselves more than the speaker. In a meaningful conversation, you have to shut up to actively listen to what the other is attempting to communicate. Try it! The next time you're in a conversation, challenge yourself and focus on how many times you had to tell yourself to *Shut up* and remain in the active listener role. It's not as easy as it sounds. However, it's vital to have a healthy, productive conversation with someone, especially if you're trying to resolve interpersonal issues.

2. **Listen with your body.** Use verbal and physical cues to demonstrate to the speaker that you're fully engaged in the conversation. Verbal cues include *yes, hmm, OK,* and other language that tell the speaker you're engaged. Physical cues

involve the use of the body: facial expressions, eye contact, a gentle touch, leaning in or leaning out, and sitting with the speaker. Active listening also works best when you're not running around the house doing a million things at once. As I say to my kids when they are attempting to engage with me in this manner for something that requires my attention, "I don't converse long-distance; please come sit with me so I can do the conversation justice by being fully engaged, not partially." Partial listening doesn't work. Vital pieces of information are often lost, leading to further miscommunications and possible conflict.

3. **Put away all technology.** Turn off your phone and put it away where it can't be seen. A device's mere presence is distracting. Out of sight, out of mind. When someone is trying to talk to you, it's rude to keep looking at your phone because it's flashing or beeping. This is a form of partial listing. It doesn't work. Off and away! It's that simple and basic, yet most struggle to part with technology even for a short time.

4. **Stop forming rebuttals and stay focused.** We are all guilty of this. When someone is talking, rather than attending to what they are sharing, we start forming a rebuttal in our heads, our comeback. Active listening can't take place if you are attending to your thoughts and feelings, not the speaker's. Stop. Refocus on the speaker. Your turn will come. Remember, at this point in the conversation, it is not about you, it is about them. It's easy to tune out and get defensive when you don't like what's being shared, but if you seek to

build healthy relationships, you need to listen actively to your partner so you can understand what they are trying to share. Focus is key to having a successful conversation. Each time an unrelated thought enters your consciousness, put up your "mental stop sign" and redirect your attention. If this keeps occurring, ask to have the conversation at a later time and be honest by saying, "I just can't focus on this right now, and I know it's important. Can we take a break and continue this conversation later?"

5. **Be mindful of your negative physical cues.** People are sometimes not in touch with their negative physical behaviors such as rolling their eyes, crossing their arms (which we do sometimes reflexively or unconsciously to show our annoyance), and other closed, defensive body language. Remember, everything you do or don't do communicates interest or disinterest to the speaker. So be mindful of the physical cues you're exuding.

6. **Do not interrupt.** Let the other person finish their sentences. Ask them if they are done before speaking. Couples are guilty of always trying to finish each other's sentences. This might be cute at the beginning of the relationship, but it isn't years later. "They never let me finish my sentences and think they know what I am feeling" is a sentiment often shared in my office. Even if you think you know what they will say, let them say it. Be patient and respectful. Your turn will come.

7. **Withhold judgment.** Actively listen to understand their perspective, not to judge. It's not about you or your perspective.

8. **Ask questions.** If things are not making sense to you, ask clarifying questions such as, "Did you mean to say that you think I was hiding something from you?" The other person might reply, "No, that's not what I meant." Questions demonstrate that you're listening but also help you to understand the other's perspective further.

9. **Validate thoughts and feelings.** Validating the other's thoughts and feelings is sometimes confused with apologizing. Let me be clear: it is *not*! It is the act of acknowledging, recognizing, and affirming another's thoughts and feelings within given circumstances. Example: "If I understand you correctly, last night's argument made you feel like I did not respect you." "Yes."

10. **Embrace moments of silence.** Silences are pauses in conversations that allow both parties to think for a minute about what is being shared. They are opportunities to breathe, gather your thoughts and feelings, and reflect. Respect the space and process. Silence does not mean it's time for you to jump in. Allow the pause to happen and let the speaker continue. If you're not sure, ask. Learn to embrace silence rather than fear it. It's OK!

11. **Listen with your eyes.** As an active listener, be mindful of the messages your physical behavior is sending and also in tune with the speaker's body language. Is it congruent with what they are saying? For example, if your partner is telling you that they are happy with you, but their eyes seem to be tearing up, the two are incongruent. The verbal

does not match the physical. Be prepared to act accordingly to the speaker's physical behavior. If the speaker starts to cry, respond appropriately. This is not as obvious as it may seem. I have worked with couples in which one starts to cry during a conversation, and their partner just stares at them, further escalating the conflict. Show some compassion and tenderness. If you can't respond with a comforting touch, then respond with the gesture of passing the box of tissues. This simple gesture speaks volumes about your presence and engagement.

12. **Reflect back/paraphrase.** This is the way to demonstrate understanding not only to yourself but to the other. Start with, "What I am hearing is . . ." or, "What I hear you saying is . ." and then listen actively to their response. It's an effective way to avoid miscommunication.

13. **Summarize before responding.** Similar to item #12, it is vital to understand what the other has said by summarizing key points so the intended message is indeed the one you will be responding to. In couples therapy, after one person has shared an experience and the other chimes in, I often hear the first partner say, "No, that's not what I just spent the last twenty minutes sharing with you." This is another opportunity to ask for clarification.

14. **Express gratitude.** Thank the person for sharing their thoughts and feelings. It's not easy for most to share intimate details and emotions with others, especially in difficult circumstances.

Now that you know more about the activity of listening, you can work on mastering the skills of receiving, interpreting, and responding to the speaker's verbal and nonverbal cues.

EFFECTIVE TALKING

The counterpart of active listening is what I refer to as "effective talking." Effective talking is a skill we need to master to resolve issues within our relationships. I define effective talking as the ability to share thoughts and feelings with purpose, meaning, direction, and clarity. In fear of saying the wrong thing the wrong way, people often waste time talking in circles without clear direction. You don't need to be verbose to share your thoughts and feelings effectively. Keep it simple!

Here are some concrete things you can do to effectively talk and share your thoughts and feelings with your partner:

1. **Gather your thoughts and feelings.** Before engaging in the actual conversation, spend some time working through what you want to convey. You need to have some level of clarity, direction, and purpose. Although this might change during your conversation, going in prepared will still help you navigate the conversation successfully.

2. **Breathe.** This seems obvious, but it's not. When people share personal thoughts and feelings, they often forget to breathe because they are nervous or anxious. There is no rush, and if you feel rushed, it's OK to continue the conversation later. Take some time to breathe. Your thoughts will be clearer, and you will be better able to share them. Silence

148

in conversations is normal and expected. However, I know from personal and professional experience that silence makes people nervous. As a result, they attempt to fill it with empty and meaningless words. Learn to breathe and gather your thoughts during the silence in the middle of a conversation. Resume talking after you feel ready to share again. It's OK!

3. **Be respectful.** No name-calling or attacking the other's perspective. Refrain from put-downs, swearing, and yelling.

4. **Use intentional language.** Use "I," not "you," language. Only speak for yourself, not for the other person. Don't tell them what they think or feel. People often do this. They use accusatory language (*you*), which puts the other person in a defensive mode, making the conversation destructive rather than constructive. For example, "*I* am feeling unloved in this relationship" will elicit a very different response than "*You* don't love me."

5. **Be clear.** Don't be verbose or abstract. Just take the linear path. As complicated as the problem may be, people over-complicate it by overstating the problem. Take the direct path.

6. **Be precise.** Don't use vague and ambiguous words or equivocate; this will only lead to further miscommunication. For example, don't say, "Someone in this family is not doing their share of work." There's no need to play games. Just name them and deal with it.

7. **Get to the point.** This is often difficult for people who are trying to avoid conflict. But as hard as it may be, just say it. Liberate yourself. Take a breath and then speak. (I will address this more in the chapters ahead.)

8. **Stay focused—or refocus.** When you are the effective talker, remain focused on what you're trying to convey to the listener. Just as when you're the active listener, you must stay locked in on what the speaker is trying to convey. Avoid getting sidetracked—and if you do, practice quickly returning your focus to the topic of the conversation.

9. **Do not lecture.** No one likes to be lectured to or talked at. Remember, any good conversation is a two-way activity. Be mindful of what you are saying and how you are saying it.

10. **Lead with your thoughts, not your emotions.** This is not to suggest you can't share your emotions; of course you should. However, starting from an emotional place is not advisable. When we lead with our feelings, we are often reactive, which produces a reactive response in return and leads to an unproductive conversation. When your emotions are in check, only then will you be able to express your message clearly and speak effectively.

* * *

As illustrated, active listening and effective talking are basic skills that one can easily master. So why do so many have trouble mastering them? As simple as they may seem, people's communication styles and patterns are rooted in complex, internal, emotional workings learned in their family of origin. These blueprints serve as their manual for communication that, at times, is faulty.

Patient: "Why can't I actively listen to her? You make it sound so easy."

Me: "It's not that you *can't*; it's that you never learned *how*. You're only recreating the communication styles you were exposed to as a child in your family of origin. You internalized them and repeat them in your successive relationships."

The same is true for me, as I will share in the following vignette.

IN SESSION WITH DR. FRANK

The first time I started to come to terms with my need to communicate effectively was in session with Dr. Frank. One day, as we stumbled onto something touching on this theme in regard to unraveling the mystery of my life and my paternally relevant dysfunction, he asked me point-blank:

"Anita, I know that your father trained you well from an early age to mute yourself. However, you have shared stories in which you have lost your shit, as you would say. Tell me more about how people communicated in your family."

"Dr. Frank, as I have shared, my family's primary mode of communication was yelling. Not much listening went on except from my mother. As soon as my father would start talking, I would shut down. I did not want to listen to anything he had to say. I only had calm discussions with my brothers and mother. Very rarely did I discuss anything with my father. He mostly lectured and yelled at me. The few times we discussed anything, it would always end the same: with him yelling at me and me running into my room out of anger and frustration. I never learned to resolve anything while living at home. I suppose as I aged and tried to take charge and be in control of my voice, I learned to yell well. I had a great teacher! My mother, on the other hand, didn't yell at all. Unlike my father, she was even-tempered, and I don't think I ever heard her yell. I guess she overcompensated for my father."

At that moment, I saw a doll in Dr. Frank's office, a beautiful one that seemed out of place, so I asked him about it. He said it was his niece's birthday present. When I asked to look at it, he handed it to me. After admiring it, my heart welled up, though I did my best to hide it. As he took it back, something feral and broken inside me lashed out at him.

"Well, that was a quick deflection," he said. "What made you focus on the doll while we were talking about your dad's temper?"

"I hate dolls." I cupped my mouth.

"What does the doll remind you of, Anita?"

"I don't know." I replied. But I did know why the doll was charged with so much turbulent energy and unresolved tension.

As he probed, asking me about my childhood toys and dolls in connection to my father, my subconscious soul rebelled. But finally, I acknowledged why at that precise moment my attention had turned to the doll.

"The doll. I remember the doll." But just as I was about to reveal everything about the mystery of the doll, my subconscious deflected, which was, in itself, psychoanalytically interesting.

"My father was depressed and struggling; it wasn't his fault, and I don't want to sit here bashing him session after session. I feel like it's all I do. He did the best with what he had."

"Look, this is not about bashing him or blaming him, Anita . . . and I get that you feel the need to defend him despite everything. I understand that. However, the purpose of our work here is to explore to gain some understanding of why you do what you do, so we can ultimately work on change and help you be the best version of yourself, for yourself and your relationships, not to mention your professional growth and development as a therapist."

"You're right. I am sorry."

"No need to be so. Tell me more about the doll and what it has triggered in you that you responded so defensively about your father."

"It was one of the most f*cked-up experiences, still f*cks with my mind today! He destroyed it. It was in Germany. I was quite young. I was only allowed to admire it and love it from afar. And it broke my heart. My mother was helpless. I knew she felt bad for me, but he was the boss. God, it was like torture. It's probably one of my most traumatic memories from childhood. I remember it like it was yesterday. I remember what that doll looked like: she was wearing a yellow dress, and I think she stood taller than me. My father propped her up on the TV so I could not touch it.

153

"Weeks prior, my parents, brother, and I had attended a carnival with one of my father's work colleagues. The colleague won this beautiful doll in one of the carnival games. Since he had no children, he happily gave the doll to me. When I brought the doll home, my father took her away from me. He told me it was too beautiful to be played with and it would remain in its box. He placed it on the TV. I was devasted but didn't argue. I remember crying in bed and my mother consoling me. I remember looking at this doll daily and wondering what it would be like to play with her. And I am not being dramatic, Dr. Frank; you know it's not my style."

"Did that day come?"

"That day never f*cking came, sadly. What did come was very traumatic. It still plays like a scene from a movie in my head. I remember it as if it were yesterday, not just the event itself but all the sounds, smells, and emotions. I guess I had done something that was displeasing to my father. I can't remember what exactly, but whatever it was it did not warrant his f*cking rage. All I remember is him taking the doll out of the box and destroying it as I watched in horror. It was a horrible day, and it's still a horrible memory."

"I am sorry you had to go through that, Anita. And yes, that's a traumatic thing for any child to have to go through. Did you ever find out why he did that or discuss it later with your mother?"

"No. As I've said, my father and I never talked about things. He yelled; I took it all in. It was only years later that I yelled back, out of frustration and anger, which did not go unpunished. To this day, I don't know what made him do that. And I have never asked my mother. I know she feels bad about it, so I don't want to make her feel worse by bringing it up.

"Anyhow, there you go! Great communication skills at play. That's so f*cked up! It's no wonder I struggled with communication issues. First, I was told to shut up, then I was yelled at, then all I did was yell back. In addition to all that craziness, I was always caught up in my parents' dysfunctional communication dynamics. No wonder I am so f*cked up—or was at least. Anyway, aren't we all f*cked up?"

"You've come a long way, Anita. I am sure your training and experiences once you left home helped you to improve your communication skills. After all, your profession requires you to have mastered certain basics of communication."

"Thank you, Dr. Frank, and yes, it has. Trust me, I have learned through my relationships with friends that that method of communication—yelling and screaming at each other—doesn't work. Of course, you've helped me greatly in our sessions to work through my anger. I wish my father had received help. Maybe if he had learned to communicate his thoughts and feelings, he wouldn't have destroyed my doll. He clearly didn't have the skills. He only knew how to express his rage through outrageous behavior. That's never going to happen to me. Being able to communicate effectivity is one of the cornerstones of my, our, profession."

"It is, and I know you will master these skills. You've already begun, from what I can see."

CHAPTER 3 WORKSHEET: VERBAL COMMUNICATION

1. What is your primary mode of communication with your partner, family, and friends?

2. How is this mode working for you?

3. What are some pros and cons that you have experienced using this method of communication?

4. Do you text your partner more than you talk with them?

5. Describe the communication style in your family of origin. How did they model communication to you? For example, my father mostly yelled at us and told me to listen and not speak.

6. Were you encouraged to talk in your family growing up?

7. Were you scared to share your true thoughts and feelings?

8. Did they listen when you talked?

9. Have you carried these methods of verbal communication with you in your current relationships?

10. Are you a better listener or talker?

11. What are your strengths as a listener?

12. What are your weaknesses as a listener?

13. What are your strengths as a talker?

14. What are your weaknesses as a talker?

15. What are you afraid of when it comes to effective communication regarding active listening and effective talking?

16. Can you agree with your partner, friends, and family *not* to use electronic forms of communication to confront or attempt to resolve problems? If not, why not?

17. How much time do you spend on social media during a given day? (Give an honest assessment.)

18. Do people in your life complain about the amount of time you spend on your phone (excluding work time)?

CONGRATULATIONS!

You're on your way to unf*cking your life and relationships by learning the basics of healthy communication. Active listening and effective talking will serve to enhance every relationship in your life, from platonic to familial to romantic to collegiate to professional.

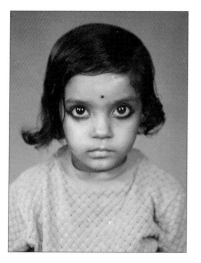

This photo of me was taken in India before leaving for Germany (I was about age three). You will notice the dark makeup around my eyes in some of these early pictures. It's called "Kajal." Indian people apply to babies and toddlers eyes, sometimes in the form of a dot behind their ears or on the forehead to protect them from the evil eye and to ward off evil spirits.

I loved playing with Play-Doh as a child; it was one of the few toys my parents could afford. This is one of very few pictures I have of myself as a child; I was probably around four years of age. This photo was taken in our first apartment in West Berlin.

My father as a young man (age unknown) in West Berlin, Germany.

This family picture was taken in West Berlin when we reunited with my father after years of living apart. From left to right: me, my mother, my father, and my older brother. I was between the ages of four and five.

Enjoying another day out in West Berlin. From left to right: my older brother, my father, my mother, and me.

Another day trip in West Berlin. I am always holding my mother's hand in most of these pictures. From a young age, I was fearful of my father. I stayed very close to my mother. That didn't change much throughout my life.

My father (on the right) in front of the Brandenburg Gate in Berlin, Germany. After World War II it came to symbolize the Cold War division between East and West—and since the fall of the Berlin Wall, a reunified Germany.

Walking up to our first apartment in West Berlin. My father was very proud that he had secured a new home for us. From left to right: my mother, me, my father, and my older brother.

This is one of the very few pictures that exists of my mother. Her age is unknown, but it was taken before we moved to West Berlin. She was and is still a very beautiful woman.

This family picture was taken in Montreal, Canada, after moving from West Berlin. I remember this picture being taken as if it were yesterday. It was after a wonderful day with the family who helped us get settled into the country upon arriving at the airport. It was also soon after the birth of my younger brother. I am ten years of age. From left to right: my father, my older brother, my mom, my baby brother, and me. Notice my father's attire; he always believed in dressing well regardless of the occasion. And notice my brother and I are dressed in the same shirt. Early on, my father had an issue with my femininity although my mother did as much as she could by putting bows in my hair. I wanted to wear pretty dresses, but he was not supportive. I guess that is why I now love women's fashion and appreciate dresses! I embrace my femininity, which was suppressed for a while. Not anymore!

These are school pictures from elementary and middle school at various ages. I don't have many of these as school picture packages were expensive at the time, and my parents could only buy them occasionally. Some of my fondest memories of school are walking with my brother. From a very young age, we talked as we walked to and from school together, sometimes engaging in mischief along the way. I used to pick tulips from people's yards and bring them home to my mother. That was as naughty as we got at that age.

Me at the Place Bonaventure grounds in Montreal, Canada, after graduating with my bachelor's degree from Concordia University in 1996. It is still one of my proudest moments. It took me six years to complete a four-year degree because I finished it while working full time and attending school at night. Only near the end was I able to attend full time after securing some financial aid.

My mother and I are on the grounds of Place Bonaventure after my undergraduate convocation from Concordia University in Montreal, Canada. It was a beautiful day, and my mother was so proud of me.

A photo of me in the educational research lab at McGill University in 1997. During my graduate studies, I was honored to be hired as a research assistant for the summer by Dr. Mark Aulls, my mentor and thesis advisor. I am eternally grateful to him. He played a pivotal role in helping me to believe in myself academically and as a woman in the world.

I'm enjoying the moment on the grounds of McGill University after convocation. I wanted that day to last forever. I felt accomplished and successful! It was an empowering experience, and I knew I had come a long way.

Here I am in 1998, receiving my graduate degree diploma at convocation. Graduating from McGill University and having my father there to witness it was one of the most emotional moments of my life. I needed him to be proud of me and his validation. I remember our embrace afterward, which was not something that happened often between us. It remains one of my fondest memories.

A proud moment with my father after receiving my graduate diploma on the grounds of Place Bonaventure, Montreal, Canada. It was a glorious day! I felt a great sense of accomplishment and, for the first time, felt close to my father in a way I had never felt before. I wanted him to know that his dreams of wanting a better life for me, the mantra of most immigrants, were becoming a reality.

This is one of the very few pictures in which both my parents were experiencing joy. It's rare that most of my younger years were spent dancing around their relational challenges, which they had many!

This unique photo is one of most cherished photos of my father. Before going to work at 3 p.m., he would often sit in the backyard and enjoy the fresh air before clocking in at the GE factory where he worked as a machinist. His work ethic was unmatchable.

I'm smiling from the inside out; it took a while, but I am here. I started embracing all aspects of myself and finally began living in the "here and now" with a healthy curiosity for the future.

Unf*cking relationships take a great deal of introspection. A healthy level of introspection will lead to self-awareness, which then needs to be used to either remove yourself from the emotional wreckage or create change within it. You choose!

Our mental health hinges on the quality of our relationships. Improve your relationships! Improve your mental health! Get unf*cked!

Unf*ck yourself and your relationships by *embracing* your inner "shit disturber"—*not* by repressing it as I tried to do for so many years!

You can look back at your past with the goal of doing things differently in your life and your current relationships. *Visit* the past—but don't *live* there.

UNF*CK MIND READING:
Needs and Expectations

COMPATIBILITY IS A KEY variable required in sustaining and maintaining long-term relationships as it determines whether our needs and expectations will be met or unmet. However, compatibility is not without unconscious interference and contamination from our childhood experiences regarding needs and expectations. Because you have been in relationships, you will not only relate to how early emotional injuries easily spill into our adult relationships but also understand the power of our emotions to cloud compatibility. Again, our "emotional blueprint," to which I often refer in this book, from childhood shapes and guides the manners with which we navigate adult relationships on every level. What does your emotional blue-print look like? Were your needs and expectations mostly satis-fied or mostly disappointed? If you experienced disappoint-ment, how were these feelings dealt with? Were they squashed or given a forum for expression? The answers to these ques-tions, and many others centered around needs and expecta-tions, haunt us in adulthood as we try to repair and resolve that which remains unresolved and dissatisfied. "He's just like my dad, always disappoints me on my birthday." "She's just like my mother, hasn't cooked a meal for me since we got married, even though she says she loves to cook and cooks for everyone else." "She never wants to hold hands or touch me; it's so frustrating, hurtful, and disappointing." These are sentiments I regularly help people work through. Despite the varying narratives, they speak to unmet needs and expectations, all leading to dissatis-fied and unhealthy relationships.

I am also confronted with people who claim not to have any needs or expectations yet experience much conflict in their relationships. "I am very easygoing, I don't need anything or expect anything, and go with the flow, so I don't know why we are always fighting." I do not believe these types of dismis-sive claims and confessions reflect their absence of needs and expectations but indicate an inability and/or willingness to acknowledge, identify, and articulate them to themselves, first and foremost, and then to others. Although, as stated earlier, compatibility serves to meet needs and expectations in rela-tionships overall, within the parameters of compatibility, we are in the service of various personalities and identities. In romantic relationships, for example, although society promotes a seamless oneness, a fusion coupleship, there are two identities that need to learn to coexist. "You are two different people," I often say to couples. "You're compatible in many ways. In other ways, you have different expectations, and that's healthy and normal. We just need to work with the difference. You are not mirror images of each other but are two identities coming together to form a relationship."

IDENTIFYING NEEDS AND EXPECTATIONS

After acknowledging that we *all* have needs and expectations and tweaking our internal blueprint to reflect the present instead of the past, the next step is to identify, articulate, and then share them with our partner, family, or friends. These steps empower us to challenge and overcome the unconscious and negative repetitive thoughts, feelings, and behaviors of our "inner child" that keep us locked up and stuck in a spin cycle of disappointing relational experiences. Each step is crucial and dependent on the other in confirming compatibility and building solid foundations for healthy relationships.

NEEDS

When discussing *needs* and *expectations* with my patients, I often start by helping them to define, understand, and distinguish between the two terms. It's my experience that people use them interchangeably and often in unison. The two, however, are very different. To illustrate my point, I refer to psychologist Abraham

Maslow's "Hierarchy of Needs" pyramid, which is believed to reflect our basic human needs. Maslow's theory divides human needs in the following manner: physiological needs, safety needs, love and belonging needs, esteem needs, and self-actualization needs.

According to Maslow, each stage must be fulfilled within the individual for motivation to arise for the next stage. Stage three's "love and belonging needs" are basic psychological necessities that include intimate relationships and friendships. Stage four's "esteem needs" include prestige and the feeling of accomplishment. Stage five's "self-actualization needs" center around self-fulfillment, including creative activities and achieving our potential. All of these needs continually overlap.

The goal in Maslow's hierarchy is to reach stage five, self-actualization, the manifestation of purpose and meaning in our lives. People's positioning on this pyramid regarding their needs will determine my point of intervention. Usually, patients present themselves to me when they are struggling with their needs in stages three and higher.

EXPECTATIONS

Now that we have a better understanding of what we mean when we speak of needs, let's do the same for *expectations*. What is an expectation? Simply put, an expectation is a belief that something will happen in a certain manner or be done by certain people. I often hear people say, "I was expecting her to do A, but she did B, and I was so disappointed and hurt." Unfortunately, disappointment seems to go hand-in-hand with expectations in relationships. It's not that one person purposely wants to hurt the other person; they don't intend to disappoint, there is just a lack of awareness of expectations. This goes back to the classic example—I still hear of today—around gift exchanges among couples, families, and friends. It's not about the gift but expectations.

"I was so hurt that, once again, I did not get anything from him on my birthday!" "She'll always tell me not to get her anything, so I don't, and I don't understand why she's upset."

It seems simple enough to solve, right? Evidently not. She was clearly afraid to be truthful about her expectations, a fear instilled in her through her family-of-origin issues and past relationships. To avoid such outcomes, she needs to acknowledge the root of the problem while working on symptom relief.

All too often, our expectations are based on nonverbal, implicit social contracts. People construct their expectations for others within their minds without ever having a conversation about their expectations. They have an unspoken deal in which the specifics—rooted in one's past relationships, individual goals, and values—are never discussed. It's difficult, to say the least, to meet unspoken expectations. I refer to this as engaging in "magical thinking." And magical thinking only works in fairy tales, not real life. Stop engaging in magical thinking and start talking to one another about what you need and expect, and then adjust accordingly.

That's not to suggest that you should lower your expectations, not at all. Those who do so risk further disappointment. In my clinical experience over the years, it's clear that people with low expectations tend to be in relationships where they are treated poorly. Conversely, people with high expectations tend to be in relationships where they are treated well. This suggests that a person is far more likely to achieve the kind of relationship they want by having high standards rather than looking the other way and letting things slide. By high standards, we are referring to relationships in which there is healthy communication about one's needs and expectations. When there is a breakdown, productive conversations bring things back to a positive relational status.

What basic expectations should we have for ourselves and others in relationships? These are ultimately personal and as such should be identified individually; however, I do believe the following principles reflect universal expectations in healthy relationships (setting aside sociocultural norms): love, trust, kindness, respect, physical affection, open communication, and the freedom to be oneself without infringing on the other as illustrated in the following vignette.

IN SESSION WITH DR. FRANK

My sessions with Dr. Frank proved to be invaluable in my

personal and professional journey since our initial meeting during my first year of post-graduate clinical training. I was beginning to feel my transformation through my interactions at the training institute with friends and with my family— even with my father. I had adjusted my expectations of him, and he had clearly adjusted his expectations of me. Although his struggles at times were more evident, mine were not. I started to understand myself more and more, specifically my internal blueprint for needs and expectations. But I didn't understand how it impacted my romantic relationships— there was only one—until I spelled out for myself how repressive my love life, or lack thereof, had been under the stern guard and watch of my father.

One day Dr. Frank commented, "We have not talked about any of your relationships with boys, or should I say, young men. Please share."

"As you know, Dr. Frank, my father forbade me to have any contact with the opposite sex. I was only allowed to have girls over and was never allowed to go to their homes. Kind of sad. I never experienced a sleepover until I left home."

"You never went out with boys behind his back?"

"Honestly, no, because I was afraid of the consequences. However, I did have a relationship with a man, not a boy. It's not something I want to talk about just yet. I am not ready. It was totally f*cked up and makes me sick to my stomach when I think about it."

We sat in silence for a few minutes. Dr. Frank looked intrigued, as if he wanted to command me to share. However, he remained respectful and probably knew I would eventually share it with him.

"OK, we can put that on hold for now."

"Thank you, I appreciate your honoring my wishes. So as I was sharing, I knew what my father expected of me, and I complied not out of respect but fear. I didn't want my ass kicked nor my mother to get in trouble for my choices."

I sighed. I dreaded dealing with something so private and intimate, but I pulled myself together and reminded myself this was a clinical process by a doctor treating me. I gathered my courage from the four winds, breathed deeply, then said, "I do recall an incident in which my family and I were at a dinner party. I must have been around fourteen years old, and there were boys my age present. I always felt very uncomfortable because my father watched my every move around them. I was forbidden to talk to or interact with boys outside of school. This was a clear reflection of my father's discomfort with my developing sexuality but it was also cultural. 'Good Indian girls don't talk to boys until after marriage'—that message was drilled into my head since as long as I could remember. The expectations around my sexuality were made very clear to me at a young age: 'Keep your legs closed until marriage.'

"On this particular night, I didn't think my father would notice, so I joined in with my other cohorts and did as they were doing, which was mostly talking and hanging out. Little did I know that my father *had* noticed. Upon arriving home, I was not only punished for 'flirting with the boys' as my father perceived it but was made to 'pray to the Indian gods' for forgiveness for behaving in such a sexual manner. I mostly remember feeling upset and crying. He made me feel ashamed of my body and sexuality, like I wasn't supposed to have these things."

"How has this impacted your needs and expectations in your romantic relationships today?"

"Dr. Frank, I never had a boyfriend. My father made sure of that. Sure, I had crushes on boys at school, but I never acted on any of those because of how I felt about myself. And I was terrified of my father. Deep down, I knew what was expected of me. I didn't like it, but what choice did I have? That only changed once I left home and met Oliver, who is now my fiancé. As you know, he's the opposite of my father, which was by design. We communicate well, and I am doing better for being with him. He's calm, cool, and collected. Nothing like my father. He helps me in keeping my cool. And we have talked about needs and expectations. With a few exceptions, fundamentally, they are similar."

"I am glad to hear that you have found a compatible partner. Do keep in mind that needs and expectations can shift over time as we change. What you expect today is not what you might expect in five years."

"All true, but as you and I know, we have to keep the conversations going. It's when the conversations stop and people shut down that things fall apart. I used to do that at the beginning with Oliver, but through our work and his support, those types of episodes are not common anymore.

"Compared to me, my fiancé's needs and expectations are basic and simple; he expects to be loved, trusted, and cared for.

With regard to specifics, well, we mostly just talk about it. And it seems to work out so far. We will see how it goes in the future."

And on that note, the session came to an end. I left Dr. Frank wondering about the relationships I had mentioned but never discussed before. I knew that I needed to talk about them with him because I had never talked about them with anyone in full detail before. It was complicated, and I had so many mixed feelings about it.

COMMON RELATIONSHIP CHALLENGES: A FUNCTION OF UNCOMMUNICATED NEEDS AND EXPECTATIONS

All relationships come with a set of expectations. This is *not* exclusive to romantic relationships. Needs and expectations in many ways are comparable to a job description or a road map that leads to building healthy relationships. When our needs and expectations are met, we are stable and content; when they are not, we are disappointed, hurt, and experience relational stress. It's not rocket science but rather common sense.

In working with couples, individuals, and families for over a quarter-century, I have identified five key areas in which people's needs and expectations are most challenged in their relationships:

- emotional intimacy
- physical intimacy
- division of time and labor
- parenting
- finances

In the following pages I will serve as your guide in helping you address fundamental relational problems in these areas so you can learn to build healthy relationships from the inside out with those around you.

EMOTIONAL INTIMACY

What is emotional intimacy? We hear this term thrown around on social media, TV, magazines, and a plethora of self-help books. But what does it mean, and how is it relevant in our lives and relationships? For the purpose of our work, let's begin with what it isn't. Emotional intimacy is not about sex. We can have sex without emotional intimacy and emotional intimacy without sex. Emotional intimacy, or EI, is *to be completely emotionally known by another person and to allow for another to completely know you emotionally.* EI requires you to be emotionally transparent. It is a key ingredient to loving and being loved. I like to refer to it as "emotional nudity." Imagine yourself completely naked in front of someone, with all your imperfections and wounds exposed, and without the desire to run and hide. This is the bedrock of all healthy relationships.

Emotional intimacy is a primary, basic human need. Most of us are born into an intimate setting and seek intimacy throughout our lives upon leaving our nest. It is our hardwiring. Stereotypically, men are perceived as wanting less emotional intimacy than women; however, based on my years of work with both genders, I believe the desire exists on both sides. The difference lies in the expression of EI. "He has no emotions and doesn't ever want to be close" is a common complaint about men from women. I am quick to correct this falsehood and reframe it: "He does have emotions but has been taught to express them in a very different manner than you do." This type of reframing opens the door for my male and female patients to self-reflect and commence their work on improving how they express, perceive, and experience emotions.

Unfortunately, as progressive as we may be as a society, men, for the most part, are still socialized to repress rather than express. Negative experiences related to repressing emotions over time create fear and build walls rather than bridges. We need to continue to encourage the boys and men in our lives to embrace their emotionality to serve them and their relationships better. They, too, have needs and expectations that must be met as part of the natural process of living a healthy emotional life.

NURTURING AND DEVELOPING EMOTIONAL INTIMACY

Before continuing to learn and transform your relationship, take a moment to rate EI in your relationship on a scale from 1–10 (1 representing the lowest EI and 10 representing the highest). Ask your partner to do the same, and then compare. Are the ratings close, or is there a big disparity? You might be surprised by what you learn.

Now let's explore some concrete steps and things to consider as you attempt to build, maintain, and nurture EI in your relationships.

Time: Emotional intimacy does not develop overnight. It takes time to build, nurture, and maintain. Be patient with yourself and others. In long-term relationships, EI can easily wane if not attended to because of the lack of time people allocate and dedicate to making it a priority. I often hear, "We do spend a lot of time together, but it hasn't brought us closer to each other." Upon further investigation, I often learn that *how* they spend this time is generally counterproductive to building EI. Quality is perhaps more important than quantity. Time is our most valuable currency; we need to spend it wisely and with purpose.

I understand time is a particular challenge for dual-income families, especially when children are part of the picture. Their "time currency" is scarce and is spent running the kids around, completing chores, and participating in family activities, to name just a few competing forces. However, quality time for the couple is still vital. A mother might say, "He always spends more time with the kids than me, but then I feel guilty about that because he should. The kids need him, but I need him also." My solution is to reframe the situation so it's not about choosing one over the other but trying to strike a balance between the two.

EI is developed, nurtured, restored, and maintained by spending quality time together. Time allows conversations, walks, and other activities that require personal interaction, engagement, and presence. And, yes, this means putting away all electronic devices!

Here are a few time-related steps to help you nurture EI in your relationships:

- Establish a daily time to check in with each other and be flexible if that needs to be shifted because of work/

kids/life. Just make sure it happens! Ask: "What does your day look like today?" or, "Do you need anything from me to make your day easier?" or, "Just checking to make sure you're OK." You will be amazed at how simple steps like this can help you feel connected to your partner. The things we do with consistency and regularity make all the difference in building, nurturing, and maintaining EI.

- Identify and share a list of activities that you both enjoy. Each weekend, take turns picking one thing on your partner's list and set aside time to do it. And, yes, sometimes we should choose to do things just to please our partner. Relationships require putting our partner first at times, and vice versa. This might be difficult for couples with children, so I suggest committing to this on a biweekly basis.

- Share the task of making the activity/date happen. The most common complaint around this is that the responsibility always falls on the same person to plan and organize the day or evening, which creates tension and, at times, more conflict. Take turns. You're both responsible for keeping the connection alive.

- Make a point of giving your partner daily affirmations and compliments. They are free!

- Greet each other with a kiss and/or hug in the morning, in passing, leaving the house, and before bed. Little things add up to big things.

- Laugh together. When was the last time you shared a "belly laugh" with your partner? It is the best medicine and connects people, and it's contagious. When we laugh, our brains release endorphins, the natural feel-good hormone that promotes well-being. It doesn't come from a bottle, and it's free!

Mutual desire: Emotional intimacy requires people to have the desire to be emotionally close. If one person is not interested or invested in building EI, the relationship will not work, and continuing it will only lead to disappointment. I have worked with many people who think the other will eventually desire closeness if they try harder, live together, get married, or even have children. When it doesn't materialize, they are disappointed and hurt. Don't set yourself up for failure; have the conversation and ask the difficult question: "Do you want to be close or not?"

Trust and emotional safety: Emotional intimacy requires building trust and feeling emotionally safe with the other person. Trust is built over time and through shared experiences. Emotional safety means you can say what you think and feel, not what you think others want to hear, without the fear of judgment.

Honesty: This important step is predicated on the two previous ones. To be honest with someone, you have to be able to trust them and feel emotionally safe, meaning you will not be betrayed and that what you have shared remains in a safe, comfortable space.

Embracing conflict: Emotional intimacy propagates

conflict. There is no way around it. We need to accept it, embrace it, and learn to resolve rather than avoid it. That's easier said than done when we are hardwired and trained to avoid conflict. I will discuss this in greater detail in chapter 6 and provide some concrete takeaways.

Confrontation: As conflicts arise, emotional intimacy requires confrontation. If you can't confront your partner about relational problems, the relationship will be compromised and possibly end over time. I encourage you to be proactive rather than reactive—take control of the problem before the problem takes control of you. Talk about it, not in the heat of conflict but later when things have calmed down. Again, I will talk about constructive confrontation in chapter 6 and offer some specific tools to help you turn a confrontational experience from a negative to a positive!

Check-up: As you walk through these steps, it is important to check in with each other every six months to a year. Set aside time to evaluate and assess whether your needs and expectations are mostly getting met. If not, talk about adjustments that need to be made on either side.

GATHERED EATING
VS. SCATTERED EATING

The idea of eating together is not new. It's a tradition that has been practiced for decades and is a quintessential human experience. The basic act of eating together personifies solidarity, fosters unity, and reinforces a sense of community. Unfortunately, the unified dining experience, to which I refer as "gathered eating," is increasingly being replaced with what I term "scattered eating." Gathered eating is fundamental to building emotional intimacy in all healthy relationships, while scattered eating works against EI and erodes our ability to make connections with those around us. Think about when we are first courting someone or building friendships. We usually arrange a date that involves eating or having a drink with each other, face-to-face, in person. We are trying to get to know the person; we are trying to build EI.

Sadly, we have allowed other activities to take its place. People are scattered throughout the house eating separately, in front of the TV, in their rooms, with their smartphones, or in the car. I believe this has severe consequences on relationships and creates feelings of disconnect within families and couples. Subsequently, I believe gathered eating is one of the most important activities we need to return to and engage in as couples, families, and individuals. Breaking bread together helps to build, nurture, and maintain EI, which is the bedrock of all healthy relationships. The process of gathered eating requires us to reserve a *time* and a *space* and has *purpose* other than the obvious of providing our body with nutrients. It also serves to feed our hunger for emotional intimacy by allowing us to connect with one another. Just as our body needs food to grow and remain healthy, so do our hearts and minds need intimate human interaction to survive and thrive in relationships with others.

In addition, the rituals around mealtime bring people together for a unique, collaborative experience. Being in the kitchen together, sharing in the operational tasks of cooking, setting the table, the discourse that ensues, and the cleanup that follows are all elements that dance in concert to unify us at the core of our basic human need to forge bonds. Overall, gathered eating serves the purpose of building, nurturing, developing, and preserving emotional intimacy. The irony in all of this is that as connected as we are today globally, I believe we are the most disconnected emotionally from the people in our lives. Hence, I am urging people to get back to the basics of love and life by practicing gathered eating and eliminating scattered eating.

I realize when you've been practicing scattered eating, it's difficult to switch to gathered eating; however, you can do it. How? First, talk to your partner and discuss that you would like to do this at least a few times a week if possible, and then make it happen—from meal prep to cleanup. If you have kids, call a family meeting and *tell*, don't *ask*, them about how things are going to change around mealtime. *You are your family's pilot!*

During these meals, all present in the household will participate in some way. Patients often complain that they don't want to eat together because their kids start fighting. I advise them to let the kids try to work it out and, if they can't, to intervene. I recommend starting off by asking everyone to share a story about their day, and no one is allowed to say it was *just* "good," "fine," "nice," or "OK." These are what I refer to as "rice-cake words" because these words lack flavor, feel boring, and are used to fill the air with nothing. They don't tell me anything. No rice-cake words at my table; make it your rule also.

I challenge you to think about emotional intimacy in your relationships within the framework of needs and expectations. How would you rate yourself? Your partner? I believe emotional intimacy is the connective tissue that creates a solid foundation for all healthy relationships. It keeps the "immune system" of any relationship strong and healthy and prepared to deal with any "virus."

PHYSICAL INTIMACY

Physical intimacy is not emotional intimacy, although sometimes the two terms are confused and used interchangeably: "We just had sex; isn't that enough emotional intimacy for you?" It is so much more than *sex*. Physical intimacy involves physical contact and sensual proximity: making eye contact, being in someone's physical personal space, sitting close, holding hands, kissing, hugging, engaging in back rubs, and all forms of sexual engagement that are not exclusive to intercourse. All too often in my clinical experience, physical intimacy is thought of more narrowly, reduced to and only associated with sexual intercourse.

Part of my role as a clinician then becomes to help broaden that scope to include nonsexual touch, which I believe promotes emotional intimacy and leads to more satisfying relationships overall. Makes sense! The more you engage in positive and satisfying touch, the more satisfied you will feel emotionally in your relationship. It's not rocket science. Simple touches communicate emotionally from psychological, sensory, and relational perspectives—qualities that are often missed via language. Positive invited touch also transmits a sense of being loved, cared for, and accepted. As humans we are meant to touch and be touched by others. It's part of our DNA. A hug or touch has physiological effects which result in the release of oxytocin, the love hormone, and a reduction in cortisol, the stress hormone.

On an individual level, physical touch strongly impacts our overall mental well-being. Conversely, studies have shown that deprivation of touch can lead to irritability, frustration, anxiety, depression, gastrointestinal issues, insomnia, loneliness, sadness, and more. Tender touches at the beginning of all relationships set the groundwork and framework for healthy emotional and sexual experiences, experiences that later can become stressful if not talked about. In my over twenty-five years of working with couples, I can attest that physical intimacy is one of the most difficult subjects to address openly and honestly.

Everyone wants to talk about it, yet no one wants to talk about it. *Why?* On the surface, it's a very private part of people's lives. However, on a deeper level, this resistance is a function of how sex was dealt with in your family of origin. In my family of origin, sex was a taboo subject. We never talked about it, and I remember feeling very guilty and ashamed of my emerging sexuality. Most of what I learned about sex was from my friends, school, and television. Subsequently, I am very open with my children about sex and their sexuality with the intent of helping them have a healthy relationship with their emerging sexuality and their inevitable sexual experiences.

In my clinical experience, most people's frustration with physical intimacy is in the following areas: frequency of sexual activity, quality of sexual intimacy, and the initiation dance that presents different challenges, some of which are expected in long-term relationships.

RESOLVING PHYSICAL INTIMACY CHALLENGES

Here are some concrete changes you can make to counter difficulties with quality, frequency, and your initiation dance footwork. However, before attempting to engage in any of the following, remember the importance of increasing overall nonsexual touch—it is key to improving physical intimacy in your relationship.

Quality. Boredom in the bedroom is not an uncommon problem experienced by couples. As humans, we thrive on variety, and if we choose to be in monogamous relationships, this force of nature can be challenging. In my clinical experience, it often is. At times, people struggling with "bedroom boredom" will cross the line of monogamy to feed their need for more fulfilling sexual experiences, which usually creates more problems than solutions.

"He just expects me to do everything." "She just lies there like a dead fish." "I haven't had an orgasm in years but am afraid to tell him." I usually begin by addressing these sentiments of sexual dissatisfactions by asking, "Have you talked to him/her about it?" It seems like the most reasonable and basic place to start, yet it's the most difficult thing to talk about in relationships. "Are you crazy, Anita? I would *never*." And then, of course, I say, "Well, everything starts with a conversation. If you can't talk about it, then how do you expect things to change?"

Communicate. Get comfortable talking about sex. Use the skills you've begun to master from chapter 3 on verbal communication. When talking about sex, *do not* attack, criticize, or judge the other person's sexuality. Use statements such as, "Do you think it would be nice if we tried . . . ?" rather than, "You just lie there. You need to change that." The latter will only generate more negativity and put your partner on the defensive. Nothing positive will come of that type of a conversation. Let's be sensitive and mindful when talking about a sensitive topic that mines the depths of our needs and expectations and those of our partner. You can't get your sexual needs and expectations met without ever having discussed them. That's engaging in magical thinking, which does not work! Talking to each other is a basic action toward resolving our conflicts, yet it is one of the most difficult steps for most, especially when it comes to sex. To work it out, we need to talk it out.

Make healthy lifestyle choices. Lifestyle choices greatly impact our sexual desire and performance. A healthy lifestyle of regular exercise, no smoking, and good nutrition is widely known to help maintain sexual health. Conversely, an unhealthy lifestyle of smoking, obesity, heavy drinking, lack of exercise, and, yes, lack of sexual activity has a negative impact. The adage is true: if you don't use it, you will lose it, and both frequency and quality of sexual experience are affected by lifestyle choices.

Increase EI. A healthy sexual relationship is built on a solid foundation of emotional intimacy. This closeness helps create and nurture desire, which in turn contributes to the quality of the sexual experience. Work on increasing your level of emotional intimacy in the relationship by following steps prescribed in the previous chapter.

Get creative. Suggest something new to your partner, such as reading erotic books before leading up to the experience. Ask your partner for ideas on how they think your sexual relationship can be enhanced. Share your sexual fantasies. Role play. Have sex in a different place or at a different time, breaking from routine. Introduce the idea of sex toys; it's nothing to feel guilty or ashamed of. You would be surprised at how many people are using them. I am always pleasantly surprised. Why not if your partner agrees to it. If you have a fetish, share it with your partner rather than hide it in shame. It can enhance your sexual experience.

Don't skip the foreplay. Make the buildup and anticipation as important if not more important than intercourse.

Engage in "afterplay." Yes! It's not over because it's over. Don't just jump in the shower or go about your business. Spend some time together cuddling or talking.

Be sexually self-aware. Before looking at what your partner can do to improve your sexual experience, take time to explore, discover, and attempt to understand your thoughts, feelings, and hang-ups about sex and your sexuality, beginning with your family of origin. Was it something that was openly discussed, or was it regarded as taboo? How do you think and feel about sex today? Are your thoughts similar or different to how your parents thought? In what ways?

Write down your thoughts and feelings about sex and sexuality as they pertain to your past and current relationships. This process of self-examination can help you gain greater knowledge about your sexual experiences, which can then be shared with your partner with the goal of improving your mutual experience. Once you have some level of knowledge and understanding of your sexuality, then you can attempt to master your body.

Master your body and mind. From working with so many people over the years, it's become clear that masturbation is still regarded as something to be ashamed of and is associated with much guilt. As a result, some have never tried it. Let me be clear: masturbation is healthy, normal, and natural, and it is the only way to know your body sexually. Own your body and, in turn, your orgasm. Yes, you are in charge of your orgasmic experience. It is not something that your partner gives to you; rather, it is something you give yourself. If you're surprised by this, it's OK; you're not alone. Most people believe an orgasm is to be given or taken like a gift, but it's not. It is you and all you in body and mind. The other person enhances and shares in the experience with you, but it is all you.

Change the initiation dance. Another common reason people cite for losing passion in their relationships is their frustration related to the initiation of sex. In psychotherapy, this is referred to as the pursuer-distancer dynamic. When a healthy interchange of these roles exists, the dynamic works. Conversely, when people get cemented in either role, the dynamic becomes dysfunctional. Pursuer: "I feel like I am always begging her for sex: she needs to initiate more." Distancer: "I would, but I never get the opportunity; he's always on me." Over time, the pursuer (asker) becomes more aggressive and critical of the other's sexuality, while naturally, the distancer (denier) becomes more defensive and distant, resulting in relational breakdown. Consequently, sex becomes associated with hostility and negativity as each partner perceives the other as using sex to manipulate the situation.

To break free from the dysfunctional dynamic of pursuer-distancer, I suggest you switch roles with your partner. The distancer becomes the pursuer, and the pursuer becomes the distancer, switching roles periodically to avoid the past (stuck) dynamic. Follow the experience up with a conversation about how it felt to be in the opposite role; identify what worked and what didn't and tweak it the next time around. Allow your partner the time and space to get comfortable with their new role. A common fear among initial pursuers in the relationship is that their partner will wait forever to initiate or pursue. It's a legitimate fear given the problem; however, I generally recommend allowing three weeks of discovery. During that time, I advise all those involved to be patient with each other. If after three weeks he or she hasn't initiated, then clearly there needs to be a further discussion about needs, expectations, and some of the obstacles preventing the roles from being played out as planned.

Frequency: Sexual frequency is related to biology and is influenced by age and stage of life. Age for men and women impacts not only sexual desire but also sexual performance. Men and women reach their sexual peaks at different life stages. Men peak at eighteen, and women peak in their thirties (some as late as forty). This also changes throughout the life cycle. Women's sexual desires decrease after childbirth and are severely impacted by menopause. Men's level of desires are affected by a decrease in testosterone levels after the age of forty, which is normal. It's beyond the scope of this book to delve into this deeper; however, it is important and relevant to note the impact gender, aging, and biology have on our libidos.

That said, research suggests, and it has been my experience as a clinician, that most sexual problems in relationships are a result of interpersonal difficulties, not biological factors. Given that, I am confident in asserting that increased emotional intimacy leads to increased satisfaction in physical relations.

If you are having issues with frequency, schedule sex! Scheduled sex is better than no sex. While it's not spontaneous, it forces you to carve out time and make it a priority. And most importantly, have an open and honest conversation about your level of sexual desire without making the other person feel sexually inadequate. Seek to understand rather than judge to arrive at a workable solution for both of you. Remember, you're not the only one in the relationship, and it's not just about your sexual needs and expectations. Be concrete. I ask couples to quantify a number and then help them compromise. Two days a week? Three? Specificity leads to clear answers and leaves very little room for misinterpretation or miscommunication.

DIVISION OF TIME AND LABOR

Most households today are dual income, meaning both adults work outside of the home. As such, successful time management and an optimal division of labor are required for households to function well. System optimization can only be established by talking with each other about what one expects and needs from the other, with the aim of reducing conflict around these issues. There is nothing like constant bickering and fighting over chores, tasks, and time to put a dent in emotional and physical intimacy and cause some real turbulence. Unfortunately, couples often present with complaints around how "time" is split up: individual time, couple time, nuclear-family time, extended family time, and social time. "Who are we spending Christmas with this year? And don't say what I think you're going to say!" "That's *way* too much time with your family!" "Oh, my God, you spent the whole weekend playing golf? What about us?" "You spend too much time with your girlfriends! What about me?" are some common complaints that, over time, can disrupt the equilibrium of relationships and pit couples against each other.

Division of labor presents similar challenges. If everyone is working outside the home, then who is taking care of the home? That's a good—and a major challenge for most couples and families today. People want the traditional outcome without the traditional means! It's not possible, nor is it realistic. The roles of men and women have changed, and neither men nor women are always clear on what they are supposed to do. Consequently, they struggle with "role strain" and "role confusion."

Role strain is experienced when contradictory behavior and expectations are placed on a person. For example, although most women work outside the home today, the majority of housework is still done by women. This is not to blame men but to highlight "role confusion," a confusion that can be easily resolved by having a conversation without judgment and assumptions, with the goal of system optimization. "I don't know what she expects me to do" and "I shouldn't have to tell him what to do: he should know by now" are frequent complaints I hear in my office.

DIVIDING TIME AND LABOR

Here are some solution-based steps you and your partner can take to minimize role strain, role confusion, and time mismanagement to reduce overall conflict over running the household efficiently, thereby shielding the relationship from residual collateral damage. First and foremost, please consider the following when discussing and creating a plan around division of labor and time management:

Availability. What availability means in this context is subjective, as illustrated in the following example. "He says he's not available to take the kids out because he's playing golf, but I think that's bullshit. I am not available because I'm working; this doesn't seem fair." Availability needs to be defined and clarified so both parties have a shared and acceptable meaning and hence make choices accordingly in a unified manner. However, it is also necessary to be open to and mindful of granting grace to your partner to make time for things they enjoy when they have a break from work.

Convenience and efficacy. These have to do with using common sense. For example, if she works from home, it may make more sense for him to do the grocery shopping on the way home from work if he drives past the grocery store, even though they're both equally available.

Energy level. Who is better equipped for the task with regard to energy? For example: maybe she gets home in the early afternoon and could mow the lawn but has a physically demanding job and is exhausted at the end of the day.

Skill set and capability. Who can best do the job? I often hear complaints about chores being assigned based on these two variables. "I can't cook, so I wait for her to get home to start the dinner. She gets mad at me, but when I have tried to prepare a meal, she doesn't eat it." My solution is to suggest that he do the prep work and they share in the rest of the task once she gets home. She has the ability and skill set to do the actual cooking, but he can take some stress off the situation by prepping.

Now that we've covered some basics of what to consider, let's look at some action steps, and remember that everything starts with a conversation:

Fixed tasks. Fixed tasks are tasks that occur regularly. Most households engage in similar tasks daily, which include making meals, driving the kids to activities, cleaning, mowing the lawn, and taking out the trash. When my patients argue over these fixed tasks, I often say, "These are not surprises. You know what has to be done and when it has to be done, but you do not discuss it with each other. Instead, you have conversations about it within yourself. Stop doing that." Engage in a real conversation with all involved, including your children, and collaboratively make a list, considering the variables just discussed, such as availability and so forth.

Variable tasks. Variable tasks are less predictable and require more flexibility. They include things such as getting the car's oil changed, paying bills, doing taxes, planning a family vacation, and occasional unexpected tasks. The only effective way to conquer variable tasks is to talk about them and decide on a course of action based on the variables mentioned such as skill set, capability, availability, and so forth.

Shared tasks. These tasks are done together and include primary and secondary rewards. For example, let's examine sharing the task of preparing a meal together through a collaborative lens. The primary reward is that the task gets done with four hands rather than two, which in most cases is a bonus because it's more efficient. The secondary reward is that the couple experiences another opportunity to nurture emotional intimacy.

Outsourcing. Know when to say *no*. Sometimes we just need to hire someone to do the job and accept that we can't do it all. Women especially suffer from Superwoman complex and might need to hear these words: It's OK to hire someone to clean the house. It doesn't mean you're a failure. It just means you'd rather do something else with your time—and time is our most valuable currency.

Flexibility. Practice being flexible. Sometimes unforeseen circumstances mean your division of labor and time allocation need to be shifted. That is OK! Accept it, deal with it, and move on.

RECIPROCITY

We can't address the topic of needs and expectations without addressing reciprocity, as these concepts are intertwined and work in harmony with each other. What does reciprocity mean, and how is it relevant in relationships? Reciprocity refers to a mutual exchange between people that is of benefit to all involved. Many people think of it as monetary items and gifts, but it extends far beyond those. "We always reciprocate with gifts on our birthday. Reciprocity is expected on those days but not on Christmas." In this example, the expectation on both occasions is clear regarding reciprocity. "I reciprocated by taking care of her dog while she was away on a business trip." This, too, represents a concrete exchange for mutual benefits.

Issues arise when mutuality is not respected. "I always send her flowers on her birthday, but she never does anything for me, not even make me a nice dinner—nothing." The imbalance created when one gives more than the other leads to greater problems in a relationship. "I love him more than he loves me because I am always giving of myself. I don't expect anything in return, but seriously." Are we keeping score? Absolutely we are, consciously or unconsciously. Those who say otherwise are in denial. We all have a mental score sheet. I believe it is in our DNA. Interestingly, research suggests that the response time of reciprocation is a function of the level of emotional intimacy of the relationship. That is, the higher the level of intimacy, the slower we are in our reciprocal response. One would think it's the opposite. You're more likely to repay a debt to your lender than to your mom.

Denying needs and expectations around reciprocity in relationships sets the relationship up for failure. If your reciprocity scale is unbalanced, then over time, this will lead to dissatisfaction, disappointment, and possibly the end of the relationship.

The good news is that this is a very common problem, so you're not alone. On the surface, some very simple and basic prescriptions can be applied:

1. Have an open and honest conversation with your partner about their expectations around giving and receiving, not only gifts but other, less tangible forms. The key is to be very specific: "On my birthday, I expect _____ (a small but thoughtful gift such as running gear; you know I am an avid runner and can't have enough running clothes)." "When I make you dinner, I expect _____ (you to wash the dishes afterward)." Simple and specific! Don't leave the conversation without having established some concrete rules and a mutually agreed upon understanding about reciprocity.

2. Tackle the root of the problem by exploring the origin of your thoughts and feelings. Apply some of the previous steps discussed in the book, beginning with self-awareness. I challenge you to think about how your needs and expectations, with regard to reciprocity, were experienced in your family of origin. Have you recreated a similar dynamic? If yes, that's the past, and your past does not have to be your present. Again, it's simple yet complicated but resolvable.

3. Lastly, have a follow-up conversation six months later to make sure you and your partner are acting according to your

newly established rules. If not, identify any shortcomings with your partner and adjust accordingly. Perhaps circumstances have changed and what you agreed to previously is no longer workable. Remember, the goal is to keep our conscious/unconscious ledger of giving and receiving mostly balanced, leading to positive relational outcomes.

PARENTING

Children bring much joy to our lives and complete the family picture, which takes many shapes and forms today (single parent, nuclear family, stepfamilies, and so forth). But coparenting adds a great deal of stress to couples' lives and often creates a divide that serves to polarize rather than unite and serves to chip away at emotional intimacy. I am all too familiar with it professionally and personally, being the parent of two children. I could devote a whole book to parenting alone, of course, but instead, I will touch on a few key points that are relevant in helping couples maintain a healthy relationship with each other. What I'm about to share is not new information; I am sure you have read it many times before. However, that doesn't mean you have applied it to your life.

On a consistent basis, I listen to couples fight about each other's parenting style, revolving around simple daily operational tasks that include bedtime, mealtime, homework, cleaning up, and other responsibilities. The constant bickering over managing these day-to-day affairs smoothly, especially in dual-income setups when everyone is trying to get out the door, creates a tremendous amount of stress. "Our kids are running the household because my wife doesn't follow through with consequences. So then I have to step in and be the bad guy, and that's not fair to me." "I am tired too. We both work all day, but I am doing the majority of the parenting." Sound familiar?

These issues vary according to ages and stages of the children involved. As a parent and professional, I can confirm that each age and stage comes with different challenges. However, shielding the coupleship/adult relationship, hence, emotional intimacy, requires you as parents to follow some very basic rules. The rules are simple, but it is the follow-through, or lack of it, that leads to great conflict between parents, which in turn generally results in misbehaved children and stressed-out parents. Their behavior is largely a function of the parents' divide, a divide that provides children the opportunity to further challenge their parents' incongruencies. This is normal and natural; children seek to maximize pleasure and minimize pain on a very primitive level.

Again, it's beyond the scope of this book to fully do justice to this topic, so I will bring attention and awareness to some core ways parenting can wreak havoc on otherwise healthy relationships: "We never fought like this before we had kids." The intent of this section is to help empower you with some basic prescriptions, with the goal of relieving some of your "couple stress" and uniting you as parents—but ultimately as a couple. From my clinical experience in working with couples, it is my belief that inconsistencies in three areas of parenting are responsible for much of the conflict, all of which are intertwined and interdependent:

1. **Structure**. All children, regardless of age, need structure, meaning a routine that includes a defined wake-up time, school time, mealtime, bedtime, and so on. Children thrive in a structured and predictable environment.

2. **Rules**. All children need rules to ensure the structure is maintained. For example, brushing your teeth at 8 a.m. is a rule to be followed within their structure. It's clear, basic, and easy to follow.

3. **Consequences**. All children need reasonable and age-appropriate consequences when they break the rules and try to disturb the structure, which most children eventually do. These consequences need to be identified, explained, understood, and followed through by children and parents alike.

That sounds simple, doesn't it? It is, in theory, but it falls apart when busy, tired parents allow the structure, rules, and consequences to erode. What's worse is when they begin to blame each other for the erosion of this structure and everything else that ensues. "It's her fault; she never follows through with the consequences." "It's his fault; he applies consequences that we never agreed upon, and then the kids blame me, and I get mad at him because they are right." I'm sure this sounds familiar. Let me help you get back to the basics of coparenting and restore emotional intimacy and harmony in your coupleship so you can be better parents, a closer family, and a stronger couple.

ESTABLISHING BASIC EXPECTATIONS OF PARENTING TO PRESERVE EMOTIONAL INTIMACY

Begin by having an open and honest conversation with your partner about parenting principles and beliefs. Ask them to share theirs. Remember, seek to understand, not to judge. These beliefs are generally a function of how we were parented. We either repeat, do the opposite, or use a hybrid model of parenting. Work together to arrive at a place of "shared beliefs." This will nurture and support you as a unified force. Children need to see and experience their parents' unity.

Then follow these steps:

Plan the structure. Sit down and concretely plan and map out your parenting structure. Structure includes day-to-day tasks that are part of a routine. I know this step can be especially difficult in a divorce or stepfamily situation. Even so, a legitimate attempt must be made for the sake of the children. All you can do is try on your end if that's your situation. Make sure by the end of this conversation, you and your partner have a clear understanding of the plan and structure.

Set rules. Establish and agree on the rules that govern the overall structure that you collaboratively mapped out and agreed upon. For example, at mealtime, the kids help set the table. This is a rule, and both parents are in charge of enforcing it even when the other parent is absent.

Establish clear consequences. Agree on the consequences when rules are broken. Make sure the consequences are age-appropriate and serve to help the child make better choices next time. This is often a stress point for parents; one parent is often stricter and harsher than the other. Come to an agreement that you both believe in.

Follow through. Make sure that you and your partner hold each other accountable for following through on the established consequences. This is one of the major issues that creates conflict between parents. "He didn't follow through on the consequences because I wasn't home." You must remain united and follow through on consequences when children break the rules. They need to experience and see that you and your partner are a united front.

Call a family meeting. Once you and your partner understand and agree on the structure, rules, and consequences, share them with your children. They need to know what they are expected to do, when they are expected to do it, and the consequences if they break the rules.

Check in. Connect with each other monthly to discuss how the plan is working and whether it needs to be adjusted or tweaked. Most plans do as children age and their needs and expectations change.

All of these prescriptions are meant to help you improve your coparenting skills, reduce stress on your relationship, and preserve emotional intimacy.

FINANCES

The relationship we have with money, like everything else, is rooted in our childhood and is complicated. The fight over money in relationships is not new, but the playing field looks rather different as couples strive to find a financial balance that is mutually beneficial in a dual-income situation. Fewer couples today "pool their finances," as was traditionally practiced. Many have moved to having completely separate finances. Everyone wants to protect themselves financially, and so they should, given the increase in divorce. I believe this adds to the urgency to discuss needs and expectations around money, yet in my experience, it hasn't. Money is as difficult to discuss as sex.

I have worked with couples in long-term relationships who have never had a financial discussion with their partner. They are clueless about their (combined) financial situation yet continue complaining about spending and saving habits in the relationship. It's a conversation that cannot be skipped. To build and sustain healthy relationships, we need to be aware of our needs and expectations around finances and those of our partners.

NAVIGATING THE FINANCIAL DANCE WITH YOUR PARTNER

Reduce and manage stress around money in your relationship by doing the following:

Examine your emotional relationship with money. Think about, explore, and understand your relationship with money. Share your experience with your partner and ask them to do the same and share with you. Money is an emotional matter. How did your parents dance around finances? How did it make you feel as a child, and how does it make you feel now? Did you grow up feeling financially secure or financially unstable?

Ignorance is *not* bliss. It might feel like it, but it is *not*. Know your financial picture from the inside out. You should know exactly what is earned, spent, saved, invested, and owed, individually and as a couple.

Be proactive. If your partner is avoiding the "financial talk," take charge, put it on the calendar, and make it happen by sharing financial facts that impact the coupleship by having a clear understanding of your needs and expectations surrounding money. Ask your partner to do the same.

Allocate funds. Identify your expectations on how you think the funds in your relationship should be divided.

Identify and understand yourself. Are you a saver or a spender? How does this play out in your relationship?

Confront income disparities. It's common for one person in a relationship to make more than the other. Although one person might earn less, they might contribute to the household in a different manner that is equally valuable, if not more so. For example, one person agrees to stay home to raise children. How much is that worth monetarily? These are all things that need to be discussed. Sometimes in the early phases of love, it gets forgotten and/or tucked away; however, rest assured financial issues find their ways back into the relationship—usually with greater negativity. Avoid this predicament. Talk about your financial needs and expectations. Remember, everything starts with a conversation.

Create a slush fund. Create a slush fund, even if it's as minimal as ten dollars. What do I mean by this? It's guilt-free spending without having to answer to anyone, especially your partner. This is to help eliminate the arguments couples have around something they bought that the other perceives as "unnecessary." It does work. As an adult with a paying job, I believe we should have a certain amount of financial freedom to buy things without feeling guilty. Simple pleasures deserve simple measures!

* * *

Over the years, I have learned that people truly struggle with identifying, establishing, and articulating their needs and expectations, let alone their partner's, but these are among the most basic things we need to know about ourselves and significant others. Although our needs and expectations change over time, the areas where most couples experience challenges remain stable, as outlined in this chapter: emotional intimacy, physical intimacy, division of time and labor, parenting, and finances. To help you get started, I've included an extended worksheet for this chapter, addressing each area to help identify, establish, articulate, clarify, and operationalize your needs and expectations in your relationship(s) . . . starting from the inside out.

CHAPTER 4 WORKSHEET: NEEDS AND EXPECTATIONS

NEEDS AND EXPECTATIONS

1. In your family of origin, were your basic needs for safety, food, shelter, and clothing met?

2. Were you encouraged or discouraged from expressing your thoughts and feelings when your needs and expectations were not getting met?

3. In your current relationships, have you discussed needs and expectations mutually? If not, why?

4. In your current relationship, are you clear on your partner's needs and expectations?

5. Are they clear on your needs and expectations?

6. As shared in this chapter, as we evolve, so do our needs and expectations; as such, write down what your needs and expectations are today. Ask your partner to do the same.

7. In exploring, identifying, and establishing expectations, we must also consider the act of reciprocity. Do you feel there is a healthy balance of reciprocity in your relationships regarding expectations? If not, why not?

8. Do you need to have a more candid conversation with your partner about this but are afraid?

EMOTIONAL INTIMACY

1. What does emotional intimacy mean to you?

2. What are your expectations of emotional intimacy in your relationship based on your definition and what you learned about it in this chapter?

3. Have you shared them with your partner? If not, how come?

4. How was emotional intimacy handled in your family of origin?

5. Are you repeating this experience in your current relationship? If yes, how? If not, how are you handling it differently?

6. Are your emotional intimacy needs/expectations being met in your relationship? If yes, how so? If not, how not?

PHYSICAL INTIMACY

1. What does physical intimacy mean to you?

2. What are your expectations of physical intimacy in your relationship?

3. Have you shared them with your partner? If not, how come?

4. How would you describe the quality of your physical relationship regarding quality, frequency, and the initiation dance?

5. When was the last time you had sex?

6. What are your partner's physical needs and expectations? If you can't answer this question, it's clearly time for a conversation.

7. How was physical intimacy dealt with in your family of origin? (Remember, it's not restricted to sex.)

8. Did you grow up in a touchy-feely family or was hugging and touching discouraged?

9. In your current relationship, are you physically affectionate through touch and other forms of physical intimacy, or is it strictly sexual for you?

10. If you and your partner switched roles between pursuer and distancer in your sexual relationship, how might that shift in dynamic affect your physical intimacy?

DIVISION OF TIME AND LABOR

1. What are your expectations about time in your relationship(s)? Answer this question with regard to time in general, individual time, nuclear family time, extended family time, and social time.

2. How were chores divided in your family of origin?

3. How did you *feel* about it?

4. What did you *think* about it?

5. How do you *feel* about it today?

6. What do you *think* about it today?

7. Is that how they are divided in your household currently?

8. What are your expectations when it comes to the division of labor? Please be very specific and as detailed as, "I expect him to cook dinner three times a week because on those days I work late."

PARENTING

1. How were you parented as a child?

2. How do you feel about it today?

3. Do you think/feel you're parenting in a similar manner?

4. What are your partner's expectations around parenting?

5. Have you shared these with each other?

6. What works? Explain.

7. What doesn't? Explain.

FINANCES

1. How was money dealt with in your family of origin?

2. How did you think/feel about that?

3. How would you describe your relationship with money today?

4. What are your financial expectations in your relationship in regard to earning, saving, and spending?

These questions should be answered by all parties involved in each area in your relationships and then shared with one another to arrive at compatible and realistic lists of needs and expectations.

CONGRATULATIONS!

You're on your way to unf*cking your
life and relationships by learning to
identify and share your needs and
expectations with the significant others
in your life. The mere act of doing so
will help you establish a strong, healthy,
and resilient sense of emotional
intimacy, which is the foundation
of all healthy relationships.

UNF*CK BLURRED LINES:
Boundaries

EMOTIONAL VULNERABILITIES and blind spots can often lead to unfortunate circumstances in the company of those who fail to acknowledge and respect emotional and physical boundaries. In the search for love, meaning, acceptance, validation, and inclusion, one can easily fall prey to authority figures with malicious intent and no regard for, or understanding of, the importance and function of boundaries. These people are often blind to their emotional wounds. They act out of these unconscious injuries and repeat, perhaps, what they experienced, attempting to resolve the original trauma. Sometimes what is perceived and experienced as *love* is *not* love but rather the exact opposite: an egregious act and a betrayal of the worst kind.

I can related to this personally because at the time I perceived it to be love because it was wrapped up as such. What did I know? I was just a girl. Years later, in therapy, Dr. Frank helped me to unf*ck it all, see it for what it was, and realize it was not what I had perceived it to be—far from it.

IN SESSION WITH DR. FRANK

"Dr. Frank, do you remember I mentioned a relationship I had a while ago and then told you that I didn't want to talk about it?"

"I do."

"Well, I appreciated you not pushing me in that session to talk about it."

"You're welcome, Anita. Are you ready to talk about it today?"

"I think I am. But I am worried that you will be upset with me, not respect me, and reject me, or even worse . . . blame me! It's a pretty f*cked-up story, Dr. Frank, but it was and is part of my narrative, one that I can't hide from any longer. I don't even want to. I need to talk about it, understand it, and accept it for what it was and not what I wanted it to be."

"Anita, I have nothing but unconditional positive regard for you and our work here. I am not here to judge you, only to help you."

"Well, it's quite embarrassing, and I don't know how to make sense of it all. I don't even know how it started or how I got involved in this relationship. I guess I feel guilty because I did have a crush on him and admired him from afar. I never thought it would turn into anything because he was so much older."

"How old were you, Anita?"

"I was fifteen. He was not only a family friend but a pillar in our community, someone I looked up to and admired greatly. I remember being in awe of him. He was everything my father wasn't in stature, personality, and as a father to his children. He and his kids often would drop by my house, or I would see him in the neighborhood."

"He was a neighbor?"

"I don't want to say, Dr. Frank."

"You're still protecting him, Anita."

"I guess so. I don't think you need to know that. Anyhow, over time our interactions became more frequent, and I grew to develop feelings for him. A silly crush and nothing more. Why would I think anything more of it? He was, after all, twenty-three years older than me."

"How did your interactions become more frequent when your parents, your father, kept you on such a tight leash?"

"Well, he would just come over and talk to us, often when my dad was working. It would just be my mom and me, sometimes my brothers. I remember feeling very special because he took a special interest in me. I enjoyed the attention."

"Of course you did. You were looking for a father figure, not a boyfriend."

"I don't know; I just liked how I felt inside when I was in his company. As I was saying, it is through these visits and encounters in the neighborhood that he quickly became aware of my emotional vulnerabilities and familial conflicts. Slowly he gained my trust as I opened up more to him about my difficulties at home. Before I knew it, I had his number and would call him frequently in my moments of darkness. I knew in my gut that this was inappropriate, but I was starved for attention from a man. He was very eager and willing, so I engaged. The telephone conversations quickly turned into meetups, and before I knew it, I was deeply involved with my heart. This was my deep, dark secret and his. 'Don't tell anyone, Anita; I will get in trouble,' he'd say. 'I love you, and I know you wouldn't want that, right?' 'Of course not,' I'd promise."

"Anita, first, thank you for trusting me with this experience, and there is so much to unpack here," Dr. Frank said, "but I will begin by saying that his actions are that of a pedophile. This is what pedophiles do, Anita. The grooming process starts before there is any physical contact. Please rest assured that none of this was your fault."

"Pedophile? Dr. Frank, do you know what you're suggesting? That's a strong word. I grew to *love* him and loved him fiercely. He was my first love."

"I am sorry it hurts you to hear this, Anita."

We sat in silence for about ten minutes.

It felt like hours to me. I was not happy with Dr. Frank and felt hurt by his categorization of this relationship. Pedophiles, in my opinion, were creeps and weirdos, which did not describe him—he whom I would not name. I still wanted to paint it in a good light even though deep down I knew there was something clearly wrong with this relationship, and I knew enough to know Dr. Frank was right, but it was hard to hear those words. After all, who wants to think of their first love as a pedophile? I didn't!

"I thought you were not going to judge, Dr. Frank. You sound very judgy right now, and I don't like it."

"Anita, I am not judging you. I am calling him out to you for his actions, which were wrong. Men who are forty years old don't have fifteen-year-old female friends. This was an abusive relationship and highly inappropriate, not to mention illegal. I know you know that intellectually, but I understand that it's hard for you to absorb this emotionally. It would imply that you're a victim somehow, and I know you never like to perceive or portray yourself as such. And this doesn't change how I see you. Time and time again, you prove to me that you're a fighter and a survivor. But please, let's call this what it was and not what you perceived it be."

Again, I sat in silence. I needed time to absorb what Dr. Frank had thrown my way. He had never been this confrontational or angry—not angry at me, but about the situation. I kind of liked it. He was defending me, caring for me, in a way I had never seen before. And I loved that he called me a survivor. That meant so much to me because I was, and I am. Never a victim—always a survivor.

"Anita, I am sorry if I am coming on strong, but there is a clear right and wrong here. I know in time you will see that. Please continue."

"It's OK. I appreciate your insight. I did love him, Dr. Frank, and he loved me. I know he did. And he never caused me any harm. He was good to me. I had never felt such love before. And I engaged as much as he did."

"Anita, you engaged because you were desperate for love and attention. He should have known better, being twenty-three years your senior. He abused his power and position. I understand your need and desire to protect him even today. But what kind of love requires you to keep secrets from the people you love, even your friends? If he had been your age or even close to your age, this would be a nonissue, and I would treat it as such."

"You're right. Even after all these years, I still feel the need to protect him. I recognize that it's f*cked. I did warn you!"

"Anita, the fact you feel the need to protect him should tell you something. You know that what he did to you was wrong. You have only thus far told me of your emotional involvement with him. I will ask you a very personal question, and please answer honestly. Remember, I am not here to judge you. But . . . hmm . . . it's clear that he violated your emotional boundaries in the worst way possible. Did you have physical relations with him?"

I was not surprised by his question; I would have asked the same had I been the therapist in this situation. I was surprised Dr. Frank had waited this long to ask.

"Yes, Dr. Frank, we were physical with each other. But before you lose your shit, please know that it was consensual. I wanted to. I had never had any sexual experiences. My body wanted to. It reacted to his touch. I am sorry. I feel like I have disappointed you."

Dr. Frank quickly jumped in as tears rolled down my face as if to save me from drowning.

"Anita, none of this is your fault. He crossed not only your emotional boundaries but your physical boundaries. I am so sorry that he was your first experience with the opposite sex."

"I was almost seventeen by then, and I wanted it, and I enjoyed it. Does that make me a bad person?" The tears continued as Dr. Frank, with great compassion, handed me the box of tissues from across the table.

"Anita, let me be clear: you did nothing wrong; you were just a lovestruck teenager. Unfortunately, he was a grown man and should have known better. And the comment about liking it, engaging in it, enjoying it—well, that is just a natural physical reaction to being sensually touched. Do you know how many young children who are survivors of sexual abuse blame themselves because their bodies reacted despite the circumstance?"

I was overwhelmed with all that Dr. Frank was sharing. Everything he was saying made sense, but I had a hard time accepting that someone I loved so intensely and for so many years would be defined as an abuser rather than a lover or a boyfriend. We sat in silence for some time. Dr. Frank looked as exhausted as I felt, or maybe I was projecting my exhaustion. Yet I felt relieved that finally, I had told someone the whole story—most of it, anyway.

Perhaps I resisted Dr. Frank's initial assessment of my first love as having pedophilic characteristics to protect my ego from completely unraveling and paralyzing me. People have been paralyzed by much less. Clearly, I was "in search of a father."

As my therapy unfolded, the word "boyfriend" would be properly replaced with "abuser." And I realized that Dr. Frank could express the anger and disgust I had repressed for years.

Over the next year, Dr. Frank helped me process and unf*ck my thoughts and feelings about this inappropriate relationship and understand that abuse comes in many forms, not just physical. As Dr. Frank had perceived, I knew this intellectually, but it took me some time to grasp it emotionally. When the relationship began, I had felt a tremendous amount of guilt, confusion, internal conflict, and shame, not to mention fear. I was not equipped to process it psychologically, cognitively, or developmentally. I was confused and conflicted. After all, I was only fifteen when the grooming process began. In essence, I had to go through a process of de-grooming as a young adult.

Looking back today, I can share with great confidence that working through this experience was the most transformative part of my therapeutic journey with Dr. Frank; he was a pivotal part of this process, and for that, I am forever grateful to him. He helped me confront my f*cked-up internal and emotional vulnerabilities related to this experience and guided me in rendering the powerless, powerful. This is the reason, I believe, I was able to unf*ck my mind and move forward in my life without much residual emotional trauma and, most importantly, as a *survivor* and not a *victim*. Through this experience, I learned about the importance of establishing and maintaining strong emotional and physical boundaries and being über-cognizant of those who seek to violate them because of their unresolved dysfunctions.

This chapter was particularly difficult to write. I thought long and hard before deciding to include it since it's so personal and painful. Very few people in my life know about it, despite it having been exposed back then in the community. That was both traumatic and a relief, but even my parents, siblings, and close friends didn't know the details. Ultimately, I felt it needed to be shared to empower and liberate others who have experienced similar forms of abuse.

TYPES OF BOUNDARIES

Sometimes we find ourselves in circumstances that are not of our choosing; and, despite those circumstances, through our choices we prevail. One of my favorite psychotherapists, Viktor Frankl, once wrote, "Everything can be taken from a man but one thing: the last of the human freedoms, to choose one's attitude in any given set of circumstances, to choose one's own way."[5] We have the power of choice; we need to recognize it and put it into action. To do that, we need a firm grasp of what it means to have *emotional and physical boundaries* and why they are necessary.

Boundaries are like force fields: they serve not only to protect us as individuals but also to provide stability and preserve the relationship. Through boundaries, we recognize and acknowledge that more than one identity exists in relationships and that all should be respected accordingly. Boundaries help determine which behavior is acceptable and which is not. They also control the flow of information, meaning they determine what *comes into* a coupleship or family and what *goes out*. Boundaries can be rigid, fluid, fused, or unclear and are a function of our culture, family-of-origin dynamics, and other successive relational experiences.

PHYSICAL AND PRIVACY BOUNDARIES

Physical boundaries are identified and established to protect our body from unwanted, undesired, and unwelcomed touch and to command respect for our personal space and privacy. This brings us to a subset of physical boundaries: privacy boundaries. Reading people's messages, logging into someone's Facebook page, reading a personal diary, and so on are all violations of their privacy boundaries and, therefore, of their physical boundaries, despite the lack of physical contact.

Privacy boundaries are rules established to differentiate between public and private information, which in today's world seems to be in a constant state of flux. With the advent of electronic communication and social media platforms—and their increasing use as means to share information—it's crucial that we establish privacy boundaries in our relationships. Social media behavior and patterns routinely challenge these privacy boundaries in various forms. Here's a case in point:

Person A: "I told you not to post pictures of our vacation on Facebook, but you did anyway."

Person B: "Well, it's my Facebook page. I can post whatever I like, and it was my vacation, too, not just yours. I don't see the big deal; it's not a secret that we went on vacation. Anyway, my Facebook page is private, so not everyone can see it."

Person A: "Yes, but that's not the point. It's my information. I don't want it on social media, and I didn't want people knowing my business."

Person B: "No, it's *our* information. Anyway, how did you find this out? We're not friends on Facebook because of what happened last time."

Person A: "I saw the notification on your phone while you were in the shower."

Person B: "What! You looked at my messages?"

Person A: "It's not a big deal."

Person B: "It is, OMG."

Sound familiar? It should! It is a common scenario that speaks to violations of privacy boundaries not only regarding who looks at what, but also the ownership of mutually shared information. Most people do not regard privacy as something that needs to be governed by rules. It absolutely does, and you and your partner need to have an agreement to guard against such violations.

INDIVIDUAL EMOTIONAL BOUNDARIES

Emotional boundaries, in contrast, refer to rules governing your emotional space and internal emotional workings. They serve to distinguish your thoughts and feelings from other peoples' thoughts and feelings. Violations of emotional boundaries include allowing someone's emotional state to dictate yours, sacrificing your needs to please others, and blaming others for your problems (while accepting responsibility for theirs). Emotional boundary violations leave you feeling stressed, anxious, guilty, scared, and resentful toward the other person and also toward yourself.

* * *

If boundaries are healthy and necessary in building healthy relationships from the inside out, then why are so many people afraid to name, establish, and, most important, enforce them? The answer is simple: they fear losing the relationship. In my experience, people are more willing to forfeit themselves and, in essence, their identity than to take this risk. This attempted "solution," over time, only serves to exacerbate their issues further and compromise the stability of the relationship. Consequently, they "lose themselves" in the other person, which results in feeling devoid of a sense of self. Furthermore, these boundaryless people live in fear of being judged and hurting others. Ironically, however, they end up hurting only themselves, feel powerless, and struggle with making decisions.

Conversely, in my clinical experience, people who set healthy physical and emotional boundaries have a strong high self-esteem, less stress and anxiety, self-respect, and report an overall emotionally well state, both individually and in their relationships, which translates to general well-being and strength.

Hence, it is clear that we need to identify, establish, and enforce boundaries as individuals, couples, nuclear families, extended families, with our friends, at work, and in every relationship, starting with ourselves. The following strategies are designed to help you as you work to establish or reestablish healthy boundaries.

ESTABLISHING PHYSICAL BOUNDARIES

Know your personal space: meaning, know the distance you're comfortable with when you're in a social situation, intimate situation, or any other. Don't let others determine this for you. Determine it for yourself.

Then identify who can be in that space: how close you stand near someone depends on the type of relationship you have with them. I stand closer to my family members than I do to work colleagues. And when you feel there is a boundary violation, it's OK to say, "Hey, you're in my space" through body language such as moving back a few inches with the hope that they will mirror your behavior.

Also identify who can touch you: touch should be reserved for people you are comfortable with. Some people are more touchy-feely than others, and if you're ever not comfortable, tell them so respectfully. You are allowed—it's your body and physical space.

Furthermore, identify comfortable touches: you need to be aware of what makes you feel good when you are touched and by whom, and define that which is acceptable.

PRIVACY BOUNDARIES

Begin by identifying what you're comfortable sharing and not sharing with others. For example, your partner may be able to view your Facebook page while your daughter may not.

ESTABLISHING EMOTIONAL BOUNDARIES

1. **Me, myself, and I.** The first step to establishing emotional boundaries is through engaging in introspection leading to self-awareness leading to a solid sense of who we are, our identity. When we are confident in and with our identity, we can recognize where our issues end and other peoples' begin in our interactions. Simply put, we start rejecting other people's shit (projections as defined in chapter 2) and refuse to take responsibility for their issues. Having firm emotional boundaries is knowing where "I end" and "you begin."

2. **Separate identity.** Acknowledge, embrace, and appreciate that you are different than your partner and thus have a separate identity. You are not them, they are not you, and your identity should not be fused with theirs nor theirs with yours. The goal is to create an intimate space in which both parties' physical and emotional identities coexist in harmony.

3. **Push back.** Uphold your emotional boundaries by saying what you think and feel respectfully. This is a reaction to someone's attempt at violating or pushing your boundaries far beyond your comfort zone. We have all encountered these "boundary pushers" at some point, and it can be tempting to relinquish our position for the sake of keeping the peace. However, out of respect for the "self," we must stand tall and

stay strong in maintaining our emotional boundaries despite the pushback. Don't say *yes* when you mean *no*.

4. **Respect your time**. Don't commit to things you don't want to do, and don't overcommit. Take time out for yourself when needed. Give up feelings of responsibility and guilt for others. And delegate when it gets too much for you.

5. **Choose yourself**. This is not being selfish. You need to take care of yourself before you are able to take care of others. It's OK.

Remember identifying, establishing, maintaining, and reinforcing emotional and physical boundaries is protecting yourself and your relationships while helping you to build and maintain healthy connections with others from the inside out.

* * *

CHAPTER 5 WORKSHEET: BOUNDARIES

1. Describe your experiences with boundaries in your family of origin—emotional, physical, and privacy.

2. Were your emotional boundaries violated? If so, how?

3. Were your physical boundaries respected or violated? Explain.

4. Are you recreating similar emotional and physical boundary structures in your current relationships with others and self?

5. If so, how?

6. If not, how?

7. How do you think/feel about this today?

8. Identify your emotional boundaries.

9. Do you say *yes* most of the time to people's requests when you mean *no*? If yes, it's because you have not identified or established emotional boundaries.

10. Are you a people pleaser? If yes, it's because you have not identified or established emotional boundaries.

11. Do you often sacrifice your needs over others? If yes, it's because you have not identified or established emotional boundaries.

12. Identify your physical boundaries.

13. Do you often feel people are walking all over you? If yes, it's because you have not identified or established emotional boundaries.

14. If so, how?

15. Have others accused you of being an "open book"? If yes, it's because you have not identified or established emotional boundaries.

16. What are your boundaries around privacy and what are your partner's?

CONGRATULATIONS!

You're on your way to unf*cking your
life and relationships by learning to
establish healthy emotional and phys-
ical boundaries. These boundaries will
serve as force fields to protect you and
your relationships from harm.
Be strong in upholding them as
some try to violate them!

CHAPTER SIX

UNF*CK CONFLICT:
Stop Avoiding and Start Confronting

BEING AWARE OF, acknowledging, and accepting that our perception of any given interpersonal interaction is our reality and ours alone is paramount to resolving conflict. Similarly, it's essential to understand that multiple realities can and do coexist simultaneously. This predisposition sets the stage for embracing what I refer to as the "3 Big Cs": conflict embracement, confrontation, and conflict resolution. The internalization of this paradigm allows for greater insight into differentiating between our objective and subjective realities and leads to building healthy relationships from the inside out.

What is the distinction between the two? Objective reality, simply put, is "the truth" as defined by our collective consciousness as a society. For example, an apple will always be an apple because collectively we have agreed to refer to this object as such. It's clear-cut with no room for misinterpretation. However, characteristics of the apple are open to subjective interpretations, such as its relative size or even flavor. It is in the realm of this subjective reality that people often find themselves stuck and, at times, paralyzed. Over the years, I have observed and listened to people trying to convince the other person that their reality is the correct one—a reality that the other should also accept and adopt. The outcome of this common type of interpersonal battle for "who owns the truth" dynamic is never constructive nor productive.

"That's not true," "That's not what happened at all," and, "If only she could see things from my perspective, she would see that I am right" are all statements I am very familiar with, as I am sure are you. This battle for the truth quickly turns into the right/wrong dynamic. "You're wrong; that's not the way it happened" or "Of course, *you* think you're always *right*," which only leads to further dysfunctional patterns of communication that give birth to the circular attack/defense dynamic. As a result, nothing gets resolved, and both parties are left feeling hurt, angry, frustrated, betrayed, disrespected, and ultimately unloved. Over time, these circular dysfunctional dynamics lead to the corrosion of emotional intimacy, which is the foundation of all healthy relationships.

"We can't resolve our problems because he never sees things from my perspective. And it's not fun to always feel like I am always wrong. I just feel so disrespected by him, and then he wonders why I don't feel close to him." Does this dysfunctional interpersaonal dance sound familiar? What kind of dance am I referring to?

THE "INTERPERSONAL DANCE"

The "interpersonal dance" is a metaphor psychotherapists use to describe how people interact in their relationships, dancing around each other and with each other. This dance is a function of the original dance they were exposed to and learned from in early childhood, that of their parents and other family members. As you have learned by now, in our families of origin, we pick up on how to attach, separate, talk, listen, fight, resolve, cry, laugh, show affection, withdraw, hurt, comfort, and love.

The answers to those questions are etched in "the interpersonal dance blueprint," which, for better or worse, serves as a makeshift, unconscious handbook for the "dance" you most likely engage in in your future relationships. Sometimes the footwork is healthy; other times, it's unhealthy and serves only to repeat negative patterns of thinking, feeling, and behaving—eventually leading to couples stepping on and over each other's feet. When the latter occurs, the pain, hurt, and discomfort are not often dealt with other than with the minimal acknowledgment that something is not working, and a decision to reengage in the dance expecting a different outcome. Why?

Often in a couple's interpersonal dance there exists a certain level of symbiosis, a mutual benefit, as they unconsciously seek to heal, through their partner, wounds originating in childhood and past relationships. It is my belief and experience that partners are not chosen randomly but are selected through the meeting of the "unconscious minds." This is otherwise known as "chemistry."

Have you ever thought about why you instantly connect with some and not with others? I believe this is a function of an "unconscious interplay" when people meet. It is a meeting of the minds—the unconscious minds! This mutual attraction is based on a common desire to resolve that which remains unresolved in the psyche. Clinically, I have experienced the unveiling of this unconscious interplay as couples share their early wounds. Through the course of therapy, they discover that they have selected a partner they *thought* could help heal their inner wounded child. When that misplaced hope is not successful nor worked through, the relationship falls apart.

Case in point: one of my patients grew up with a depressed mother and presented with a history of failed relationships. Through our work together, it became evident that he was only attracted to and dated depressed women, like his mother, because he very well knew his role in those types of relationships. He was a magnet for them, and they were for him. He sought to comfort them in their depression, and they were drawn to the comfort he offered. Their interpersonal dance was successful as long as they both remained in their respective roles. Any attempt to pivot or shift from these roles disturbed their relational equilibrium and neither was equipped to embrace, confront, or work through conflict.

Now that you have a clearer understanding of the interpersonal dance, I challenge you to think about your interpersonal dance and the type of people with whom you have had chemistry in the past and present, and consider how they have (or have not) served to help you deal with your wounds. Perhaps you can relate to the preceding vignette except that your relationships have not ended as his did. Yet you experience frustration as you seek to change your footwork in the dance whenever you experience resistance from your partner who unconsciously seeks to maintain it as it's the only dance they are familiar and comfortable with. Resistance is normal and expected when we are being challenged to change our emotional footwork. However it is possible! Continue reading and follow my lead.

Let's begin by identifying your interpersonal dance around conflict. Which of the following best describes you and your partner?

1. Both partners yell at each other.

2. One partner yells at the other while the other withdraws.

3. Both partners withdraw.

Note, all three interpersonal dance dynamics are dysfunctional and serve to perpetuate the conflict, keeping the couple stuck in a repetitive negative pattern of right/wrong and my reality vs. your reality dynamic.

IN SESSION WITH DR. FRANK

I first came to the seemingly counterintuitive conclusion that right and wrong are not mutually exclusive in a therapy session with Dr. Frank. One day he saw that I was struggling with the fact that while my father had the best intentions, his words and actions had the exact opposite effect. His behavior did not feel anything like love; it felt oppressive and caused internal chaos. Somehow, as all good therapists do, Dr. Frank seized upon the crux of my preoccupation by igniting the spirit of my battle with a rather keen question.

"Is it logical to assume that from opposite and diametrically opposed points of reference in space and time and, thus, from reciprocal points of view, you were a nine while your father was a six?"

"Dr. Frank, that's a rather complicated way of asking a simple question. I didn't know this was a math class. Since when are you so verbose?"

He smiled. "You're not the only complicated person in the room."

"Very funny. So that is interesting. You're saying we were, in mathematical terms, the flip side of each other?"

"Yes, picture how a nine flipped over becomes a six."

I did just that and appreciated Dr. Frank's attempt at making his interpretations more concrete. "I love it. I was the nine and he was the six, and we never met in the middle nor ever contemplated how it would look from a different angle. As you already know, we never saw much from the same perspective.

It's like we lived on completely different planets and shared a completely different reality. I think we would even disagree on objective truths. I often felt he argued with me just for the sake of arguing. I could say the sky is blue, and he would say it's pink."

"What about your role in keeping this dynamic alive by doing the same to him?"

"Oh, now you're on his side. Why didn't he try? He was the parent! Wasn't that his job: to teach me, to model to me? Seriously, now you're blaming me!"

"Not at all, I am merely pointing out your role in this type of unhealthy interaction with your father."

"Yes, but shouldn't he have known better? Why was I responsible for changing that?"

"I didn't say you were, Anita."

"OK, Dr. Frank. I get it and yes, later as a young adult, I could have worked on that, but I was stubborn like him. I was angry and unable to see beyond those emotions. Are you forgetting how old I was when all this was going on in my life? At that time, my perspective, my suffering, was the truth as I saw it. Thank god I never had this issue with my mother."

"Why, do you think?"

"Because she listened to me. She tried to understand my reality and realized it was different from hers but didn't try to tell me what it was. If we stick with your 9/6 analogy, she and I were always able to see the flip side—and still are. We had a very healthy interpersonal dance and were mostly in sync. My father and I were entangled in a very dysfunctional dance. Did you miss that, Dr. Frank? We were always stepping on each other's toes. With my mother, it was never a matter of right or wrong but of understanding differences. The nine and six could coexist, as do different realities."

"Anita, I haven't missed anything, and clearly, this makes you angry. You sound angry to me and that's OK; you're allowed to be. Part of my job is to confront you with what I am seeing, hearing, and experiencing."

"Nothing more to share on this, Dr. Frank; you know the rest. Only when I could see my father as an adult and not as my father did I understand why it was so difficult for him to shift perspectives. He was only doing what he knew how to do from his family of origin. Isn't that what we all do? Rinse and repeat?"

"I hope through our work together and your training, you will do better and will not repeat."

"Never. I will never do that with my kids. I never want to be that parent. But as you and I both know, some things go on autopilot, driven by our unconscious mind. Anyhow, it seems like I am not the only one struggling with these kinds of issues. Last week, I worked with a couple whom I think had a similar bully dynamic. I had a major headache after the session! He spent most of our time trying to prove he was right and she was wrong. I had to intervene a million times."

"That's part of your role, Anita."

"I am working on getting them to change their dynamic. They are stuck. They need to open their eyes, and I know it takes time."

"Patience on your part as their therapist is essential. You can't play into their dynamic of bullying by bullying them into seeing things from your perspective. They have to believe that what you're selling for the change is long-term and sustainable."

"Thank you, Dr. Frank, I know that already! I am not stupid, you know."

"I never said you were. I am not your father, and I know you know that. I am only supporting you in your interventions."

"I appreciate that, and I am sorry. I know you're not my father. I know it intellectually, but I can't help but feel like you embody him at times when you start giving me advice. I don't want to get into that right now."

"Anita, I'm glad you're able to recognize your projections and experience me as who I am: your therapist and not your father. Although, at times, I know as you do, part of the therapeutic process includes dealing with patient projections and providing a corrective emotional experience, meaning that you can project whatever you want on to me. It will not be dealt with as it is in the world beyond my door."

"Yes, I agree and have learned about that during my training and in here with you as the patient. Thank you for pointing that out and clarifying it. Getting back to my work as a therapist, couples work is proving to be so different from my work with individuals. Although I love both, they are just different."

"They are. What are the challenges?"

"Couples come in, always wanting me to validate that one is right and the other is wrong. I assure them that it's not what I think that matters but what their partner thinks and feels and how that impacts their relationship. And if you're in a relationship and feel like you're always right or the other is always wrong, consider this: no matter how you play the game to win or how hard you try to be right, in the end, the truth is it will always be a short-term gain, and a long-term lose/lose. For both of you." With some more bantereing on my part, the session came to an end. I left feeling more empowered as a "therapist in training" with regard to my work with couples and dealing with the whole right/wrong dance.

CHANGING THE INTERPERSONAL DANCE

Based on what you have learned thus far having identified your interpersonal dance, it's now your turn to choose the steps you're going to take to change that dynamic. Here are some prescriptions to get you started.

Shift your perspective. Recognize and accept that people view circumstances and conflicts from various angles and that those angles determine their understanding of the situation. Shift your perspective so you're able to see the problem as they see it. In doing so, you will have greater understanding, compassion, and sympathy for their perspective, which will lead to a path of healthy dialogue.

The following illustration is a perfect example of how things can appear very differently depending on where you're standing; stand to the left and it's clearly a "six," stand to the right, and it's clearly a "nine."

Change your language. Drop absolute terms such as right/wrong and never/always from your vocabulary. They are

Both realities are true and can coexist in a healthy manner. It is ultimately about being able to see and understand the situation from the other's perspective. It is not about being right or wrong.

polarizing, paralyzing, and destructive in relationships, keeping people locked in perpetual negative circular arguments. As long as you think you're right, then by default, it makes the other person wrong—and no one wants to be wrong. The more you try to prove you're right, the more the other person will try to prove you're wrong! Drop those words from your vocabulary. Replace them instead with phrases such as, "I have a different perspective on that," or, "I see you have a very different view of that." This sets a much different tone, one that is constructive, not destructive. Instead of broadly claiming "always" or "never," provide specific examples and remain evidence-based.

Drop the rope. Disengage from the "tug of war" dynamic by putting the rope down. Without engagement, this dynamic cannot exist. Holding tightly to your view while tugging back and forth is exhausting, destructive, and only serves to recycle an unhealthy relational dynamic. The more you pull, the harder the pull will be on the other side until someone drops the rope.

Remove your armor. Get ready to engage in an open conversation with your body and mind. You're not preparing for battle but a collaboration. Be mindful of the messages you send via your body language; uncross your arms and relax your body and mind through some simple breathing exercises. Yes, it does work. I practice these rituals when I am getting ready for a difficult conversation. Remember, as mentioned previously, we communicate not only with our words but also with our body language. What is your body language saying? What narrative are you telling yourself about the conversation that's about to take place? These will determine to a large degree if the interaction will be successful or not.

Avoid the attack/defense dynamic. You are in charge of your steps in the interpersonal dance, whether to eliminate or perpetuate it. Change your role and change the dynamic. The attacker cannot exist without the defender, and the defender cannot exist without the attacker. Both rely on the other to keep this dysfunctional dance alive. Which one are you, the attacker or the defender? Not sure? Think of the last time you were in engaged in this dynamic and the words you used to share your thoughts and feelings. Were they accusatory, taking your partner to task? If so, then you are most likely the attacker. Did you dispute, interrupt, and try to justify your perspective? Then you are probably the defender. Identify your role and then implement the prescriptions outlined in chapter 3 on verbal communication. Active listening and effective talking will relinquish you from polarized positions.

Seek to understand and not to judge. Use your newly learned active listening skills; when we do so we are seeking to understand the other's perspective. Understanding is key to building empathy and reducing negative feelings.

Agree to disagree. Sometimes we just have to agree to disagree, nothing less and nothing more, if we want the relationship to be successful. This can be a viable option as long as the subject isn't a deal-breaker disagreement—for example, if one partner wants to have children and the other does not. The following vignette will help you understand how I implement some of these prescriptions in dealing with my conflicted relationship with my father through the guidance of Dr. Frank.

IN SESSION WITH DR. FRANK

When my relationship with Oliver was ready to move to the next step after a few years of dating, I was delighted and ready to make the commitment. But it felt wrong not to have my family be part of the celebration, particularly my father, whom I hadn't seen or communicated with for a few years. Oliver felt my ambivalence, and it was disturbing enough for him to take action. Having come from a family different from mine in every way, he couldn't fathom the idea of having a wedding without my father, the only member of my family he had yet to meet.

While I knew it needed to happen, I feared the confrontation and my father as much as I had years before as a sixteen-year-old girl. Still, I knew that my fiancé would serve as the bridge to reconciliation with my father. I shared the story of what happened with Dr. Frank.

"I didn't have much to do with arranging it," I told Dr. Frank. "It was all between Oliver and my mother. As you know, my mother and brothers have always loved Oliver and welcomed him with open arms since day one. My mother was thrilled that we were going to get engaged and that Oliver wanted to meet my father. Apparently, they talked about it."

"So what happened? How did Oliver and your father finally meet?"

"My parents had this little booth at their local market every Sunday. One weekend Oliver visited their booth. He spoke with my father, then my mother told my father that he was my fiancé-to-be and apparently, they proceeded to discuss the reconciliation. From what Oliver told me, it was pretty positive, although my father was very businesslike about it."

"What was your father's reaction? You seemed to have fast-forwarded through a great deal of emotions. Your father, whom you hadn't seen for years, met your fiancé-to-be, and they discussed a reconciliation; it was that simple?"

"On some level, it was. Don't forget my father was much older and it had been years. I guess his anger had subsided and he was ready to meet. My mother shared that he'd expressed concerns about my welfare and missed me at times. I am his only daughter, after all."

"OK, how did you feel after Oliver returned to you with this news?"

"I was full of mixed emotions. Of course, I wanted the reconciliation to take place and finally have closure. Cutoffs, as you know, are not healthy emotionally. I feared that he would die and I would never see him again. I didn't want that. Don't get me wrong; as much as I was happy, I was also terrified."

"What role did your mother play?"

"She and I talked about it, and then I shared the plan with my brothers. They were happy to hear that this was finally going to happen. They established a time and day. It would be Saturday at 12 p.m."

"How did you feel leading up to that Saturday?"

"I desperately longed for reconciliation, all the while worried immensely about the potential collateral damage that could ensue. As the days dwindled and the time drew near to face my father again, I was afraid it would be that same damn dance with him again. What if he lashed out? Sure, I would deal with it, but would it not wound me? How much? How long would I have to grieve again? At times I wanted to hide in my hole. I feared my regression, but I knew I was stronger than I had ever been and that I would have the support of Oliver and the rest of my family. I was no longer that little girl, although I wondered if she would emerge at the sight of him. And I sometimes felt, and still feel, the brunt of the pain he caused me. I am not sure that will ever leave me. Maybe not. What do you think, Dr. Frank?"

"Anita, as you know, you have worked a great deal on confronting your issues, embracing them, and working on resolving them. However, that little girl will always live inside of you as your inner child. We all live with our inner child. The key difference is that as an adult we are in control of them, not vice versa. That's the way it should be, anyway, even though some people are governed by their inner child as adults."

"Yeah, I get it. I keep her in check as much as I can. She is not going to ruin my adult life. I'm in charge of her. She is not in charge of me. No way."

"It's the way it should be. OK, so tell me about that day, the day of confrontation and reconciliation."

"On that Saturday, as we walked up the very same driveway that I had run down years earlier, I tried to remain strong, but on the inside, I felt like a terrified little girl. At the front door, Oliver had to extract his hand from my iron grip to ring the doorbell. My heart was pounding in my chest.

"When the door opened, we were greeted by my mother's warm smile and hug. She looked a little fearful too. Who wouldn't be, given the circumstances? Oliver was the only one who seemed confident. I guess that's one of the things I love about him the most. He's always über-positive. As we walked in, I could see my brothers and then my father standing behind them. As soon as we made eye contact, I looked down. Interesting how we resort to old behaviors.

"Once inside, my father and I hugged as the rest of my family watched with tears. As our embrace broke, I quickly followed my mother into the kitchen and left my father with Oliver and my brothers. Even though we were finally reunited, I was still afraid and nervous and maintained my emotional distance. I had lived in fear of this man for most of my youth."

"I know you had, but it sounds like he was happy to see you and you, him."

"I was, and I also felt kind of sad."

"How so?"

"Well, he wasn't this fierce man anymore. He had aged and seemed to be a little frail. I knew he would be but being confronted with it felt very different. *Sad* is a good word to describe it. I didn't dwell on that feeling too long because I was super happy overall. And before long, my dad and Oliver were sharing stories and laughing. My father had always been a great storyteller to those outside of the family."

"How was your mother during this confrontation?"

"We were good. She was pleased as any mother would be to have her family back together. I asked her how all this had happened so quickly, and she shared that my father had wanted to see me for quite some time but that his anger and pride prevented it. And he was very happy that I found someone who, despite not being Indian, met his standards education-wise and in other ways."

"Did Oliver follow through with his intention that night or later?"

"It was that night that he asked my father for my hand in marriage, and, of course, my dad gave him his blessing. At this point I think he was just happy that I was getting married and that I seemed to have chosen someone to his liking."

"How did you feel finally ending the cutoff and beginning the work of resolving things with your father?"

"I was thrilled but knew we still had a lot of work to do on our relationship. It was a start. I am certain we were both aware of various realities, but I was ready to embrace whatever conflict would ensue and work on resolving things with him. I knew that would, on some level, involve accepting him for who he was. And I hoped that he would finally accept me for who I was. I knew we had a lot more progress to make, but at least we were on speaking terms. Finally, a huge load had been lifted off my back."

THE THREE Cs

If you spend enough time with someone, eventually, you will experience some level of conflict. Intimacy breeds conflict, and conflicts require acknowledgment and then confrontation to arrive at resolutions if only to "agree to disagree" if relationships are to move forward in a healthy direction. Here is an example of this dynamic in action:

Patient: "We had very little conflict at the beginning of our relationship. Now we fight so much more about the stupidest things."

Me: "Of course, it was the honeymoon phase, and now that you are both more intimately connected, it's normal to have conflict. How do you attempt to resolve it?"

Patient: "We both yell at each other and then the next day pretend like nothing happened. I try to talk to him, but he always says he's fine, so I leave it."

Me: "How is this working for you?"

Patient: "It's not because the same shit keeps happening over and over again with no resolve!"

Me: "Let's work on changing that dynamic."

As illustrated here, conflicts generally arise more frequently in later stages of relationships. As people begin to feel more comfortable revealing their "authentic selves," their responses to conflict will either decrease, increase, or force their level of emotional intimacy to remain the same. Consequently, how you handle conflict determines the future stability and longevity of the relationship.

The key to dealing with conflict in a productive and healthy manner can be broken down into three steps: conflict embracement, confrontation, and conflict resolution. Let's look at each in turn.

THE FIRST C: CONFLICT EMBRACEMENT (CE)

The first step in resolving conflict is getting comfortable with the idea of embracing it rather than avoiding and pushing it away as most are inclined to do. Avoidance is a faulty solution that only serves to perpetuate and escalate problems. Ultimately, the avoidance itself becomes the problem and is responsible for giving birth to anxiety, stress, and sometimes depression.

Patient: "I don't know why I am so anxious lately. I'm having trouble sleeping."

Me: "Is there something that's worrying you?"

Patient: "No, but I have been trying to avoid talking to my wife about some issues we are having. She never wants to hang out or spend time with me anymore. It's not a big deal . . . I just keep myself busy. I figure eventually it might go away, and things might change."

Me: "Could it be the anxiety is because of marital issues, and you're more worried about them than you're leading me to believe? And underneath the surface, you know that avoiding the conversation will not make the problem go away or resolve itself? On the contrary, it will most likely exacerbate it."

In this scenario, it's clear that his anxiety and sleep disturbance are a function of his relational problems. The patient's attempted solution of *avoidance* is clearly not working for him; it's working against him. I worked with him for many sessions before he felt comfortable with the notion of conflict embracement. CE is learning to reframe conflict as a positive reoccurring dynamic, and experiencing it as a twofold opportunity: first, an opportunity for individual relational growth; second, an opportunity to further build, nurture, develop, and maintain emotional intimacy. Once you're able to think about conflict differently, you can progress to the next step and, of course, as stated throughout these pages our frame of conflict is a function of our family of origin as with most things.

THE SECOND C: CONFRONTATION

First and foremost, I encourage you to reframe the term "confrontation." Confrontation is nothing more than the meeting of two opposing forces; it need not be hostile or aggressive and result in a fight. Similar to our initial instincts in wanting to avoid conflict, we deploy our most primitive and best defense mechanisms—such as displacement, denial, and passive-aggressive behaviors—to avoid confrontation. Most people try to bypass confrontation by triangulating another person in the conflict, thereby hoping to dilute and reduce their anxiety. This strategy serves to relieve some stress through venting; however, it falls short of working toward resolving conflicts. In many ways, triangulation further complicates the situation if the third person knows the other party. This is a short-term solution to a long-term problem. Confrontation needs to take place between the people involved in the conflict without the contamination of others who may have their own agendas. Unless it's in the company of people who are there to support a mutually beneficial outcome, leave them out of it!

Confrontation is a call to action and a request for emotional transparency. I am confident that once you've mastered the effective communications skills outlined in chapter 3, you will be ready to engage in confrontation with a certain level of compassion and understanding. Remember, your approach is key to moving the confrontation to a place of conflict resolution.

THE THIRD C: CONFLICT RESOLUTION (CR)

When it comes to healthy conflict resolution, my clinical experience with couples in recent years has led me to develop what I refer to as the "tabling method." I have been sharing this method with patients for several years and have helped many make great strides in turning their unhealthy interpersonal dance around. Tabling is simple enough to understand and easy enough to apply to all relationships.

I believe we all have an internal *emotional table* that is used as a placeholder for our unresolved conflicts. When conflicts in our relationships repeatedly go unresolved, they get stored in abstract boxes and placed on our emotional table. Over time, as these boxes of unresolved issues pile up, the table becomes overloaded and collapses, at which point unresolved issues from the past and present spill out and create further stress and tension. The contents of all the boxes become cluttered and enmeshed, at which point neither partner can identify, let alone resolve, what they were fighting about.

"Why are you bringing that up? It happened five years ago and has nothing to do with what we are talking about today." "Because we never talked about it, like we never talk about anything, so the shit piles up."

The collapse is a direct result of people's inability to communicate effectively, their tendency to avoid conflict and confrontation, and poor conflict-resolution skills. How can you stop your emotional table from collapsing, prevent an escalation, and resolve your issues, one box at a time? By following my "table it" method.

PREREQUISITES FOR USING THE TABLING METHOD

1. You and your partner agree to commit to using the tabling method 100 percent.

2. You and your partner both have a clear understanding of the process outlined here.

3. You and your partner both have a clear understanding of the structure outlined here, meaning clear boundaries surrounding the physical setting (time, location, and privacy).

ANITA'S TABLING METHOD FOR CONFLICT RESOLUTION

The next time you're in a situation with your partner that you feel is escalating, apply the following steps for tabling:

Use your mental stop sign. When you put up your mental stop sign, you stop engaging in escalation. And if your pattern in this dynamic is to withdraw and leave the room rather than take a healthy break, don't! Be present and remain calm. Remember, your action will create a reaction; whether it's a positive or negative one depends on your choice in the moment.

Press the pause button. Take three deep, intentional breaths. In an emotionally charged situation, our breathing becomes rapid and intense, sometimes throwing us into a state of panic. Instead, slow the body and mind down by controlling your breathing. Remember that our *physiology* is impacted by our *psychology* and vice versa.

Table it. Once you are calmer, say the words "table it" to your partner. Based on your agreement to utilize the tabling method, your partner is required also to put up their mental stop sign and follow suit. Mutually agree to table it.

Walk away. Give each other some space to calm down and process your thoughts and feelings. Do not chase or pressure the other to talk about the escalation at that point.

Follow the 24-hour rule. Once you've agreed to table it and are both calmer, come back together and agree on a time and place to discuss the issue within twenty-four hours. The location for the discussion should be a private, neutral setting in which both parties feel comfortable sharing their thoughts and feelings. Setting a specified time and place will ease the anxiety of the person who craves an immediate discussion and resolution, knowing there *will* be a scheduled opportunity for their thoughts and feelings to be expressed and heard. *You must follow the twenty-four-hour rule!* Why twenty-four hours? I believe that is enough time for all those involved to become more rational and less emotional; cooler heads do prevail. Sharing your emotions is very different from being driven by them in a conversation. For circumstances beyond your control (one of you has a long shift at work the following day, for example), allow forty-eight hours *maximum*.

Table it. Once the time and place have been established, you will agree *not* to bring it up until that time. If one person attempts to talk about it in the interim, kindly and simply remind them by saying, "It has been tabled. Period. End of discussion."

Journal it. If, in the interim, thoughts and feelings arise that you would like to share, write them down. Some people are better at expressing themselves in writing. A journal also serves as a container for thoughts and feelings for partners who have a difficult time waiting for the "table session." Never underestimate the therapeutic power of journaling.

Have the table time discussion. Once you are at the table, within twenty-four hours, share your thoughts and feelings about the episode using the tools you have learned thus far in this book, such as the effective communication skills covered in chapter 3. Time at "the table" should not exceed one hour. In my experience, talking about emotional issues for longer than an hour is physically and emotionally exhausting. This time limit also serves as a safeguard to prevent one partner from emotionally drowning the other. If more time is needed, continue the conversation again within the next twenty-four hours, following the same guidelines.

Strive for a win/win situation. The goal of the discussion at the table is to arrive at a mutually beneficial outcome. No one should leave the table feeling a sense of loss. And at times you might just agree to disagree respectfully. Being able to do that in a relationship is a sign of tremendous personal and relational growth in that you have liberated yourself from the right/wrong and attack/defense dance.

Confirm the resolution. Before leaving the table, ensure both of you are as satisfied as you can be with the discussion and outcome and are ready to move forward. Removing that box off your emotional table will make room for the next one. The goal is not to have an empty emotional table but one on which the boxes keep rotating.

* * *

Over time and with much practice, you will find yourself saying "table it" less often while participating in frequent, healthy conversations as a result of your much-improved overall skills in building healthy relationships from the inside out.

* * *

CHAPTER 6 WORKSHEET: THE INTERPERSONAL DANCE

1. Do you avoid conflict or attempt to confront it?

2. How do you feel about confrontation?

3. How was conflict dealt with you in your family of origin (avoidance or confrontation)?

4. Did you learn how to resolve conflicts in your family of origin, or were disagreements swept under the rug?

5. If conflicts were confronted, what did that process look like? Are you repeating that dynamic in your current relationships? If yes, how? If no, how is your process different today?

6. In this chapter, you learned about three types of interpersonal dances. Which of the following best describes your dance during a conflict?
   Both partners yell?
   Both partners withdraw?
   One partner yells, and the other withdraws?

7. Are you a person who seeks instant resolution?

8. Is your interpersonal dance similar to the one you saw modeled by your parents in your family of origin?

9. Do you find yourself thinking and using terms such as "right" and "wrong" in trying to understand a situation?

10. If so, how would you like to change your dance footwork?

11. Are you afraid to confront your partner?

12. Are you afraid of being confronted yourself?

13. What's the first thing that comes to mind when you think about confronting someone in your life with whom you have an issue?

14. How do you resolve conflict in your relationships today?

15. Do you use texting versus a verbal conversation as a primary mode of communication when important issues need to be discussed?

CONGRATULATIONS!

You're on your way to mastering the
Three Big Cs and changing your inter-
personal dance. Your new footwork
will liberate you from the unhealthy
negative, repetitive internalized
patterns of your past and help you build
healthy relationships from the inside
out in the present and future.
You will finally be able to choose
emotional liberty over fear.

UNF*CK HAPPINESS:
Forgiveness, Acceptance, and Contentment

GRADUATING FROM MCGILL University in Montreal was one of the proudest moments of my life. It was a day I had dreamed of for many years and often wondered if it would ever arrive. It did, through hard work, determination, and commitment. It is etched in my mind as if it happened yesterday.

Loud bagpipes led the students' procession from Redpath Hall to the convocation tent located on the lower campus field. As we entered the giant tent, the sight of some 5,000 people—family, friends, alumni, and faculty—brought immediate perspective to my academic journey. I was directed to my seat and sat down as the Chancellor welcomed everyone and set a positive tone for the ceremony. He made sure to acknowledge the high bar that students and faculty continue to develop at McGill. Soon after that, the chain of valedictorians began delivering their speeches. Their comments ranged from emotional to raucous. It was thrilling to know that the next phase of my life was right around the corner. I was making progress in my life, and things had come full circle. I had worked incredibly hard to get to this moment and began to reflect on my journey and all those who motivated and supported me along the way.

Upon hearing my name, I walked to center stage and paused in front of the Chancellor. She tapped my shoulder with a wooden stick; I like to think of this time-honored tradition as the university equivalent of being knighted. Then I made my way over to the Dean and shook his hand before stepping offstage where I would receive my diploma. This area is where families position themselves with cameras, ready to snap pictures. After being handed my parchment, I looked up to find my father standing next to my mother and two brothers, accompanied by Oliver and his parents.

As the ceremony ended and the Canadian national anthem began to play, I took one last moment of self-reflection before heading to find my family. I was proud of myself for having enough determination and resilience to summit this towering mountain. I had reached a pinnacle of academic achievement. To wear that gown and walk across that stage was a powerful, pivotal, and emotional moment that brought me to tears. I gathered my thoughts and stepped into the sea of people surrounding us.

As I made my way through celebratory herds of jubilant parents, my mother rushed up with open arms to envelop me. Tears of joy streamed down her cheeks, and my two brothers joined us in a huddle. As we slowly released one another, my father moved in to embrace me. His eyes were teary and his demeanor reflective as he uttered words I had thought I might never hear.

"I am very proud of you, Anita. You've come a long way. This is why I brought you here, to this country. McGill is one of the best universities. I know I haven't said it much, but I do love you and accept you. Clearly you are doing many things right."

As you might imagine, I was overcome with emotion. This was the first time in my life that my father had acknowledged my hard work, expressed his feelings of love for me, and finally accepted me for who I was and not who he wanted me to be. It seemed that he had finally forgiven me for not meeting his cultural expectations and perhaps himself for not meeting my paternal needs. Anyhow, all I knew for sure was that I had been waiting for this moment for as long as I could remember. Many times during our cutoff, I had tried to convince myself that I didn't need him or his validation, but deep down, it was what I craved the most—and there it was. I was thrilled and relieved. Despite our earlier reunion and reconciliation (thanks to my mother, brothers, and Oliver), interactions with my father always made me feel anxious, as they could go either way, even in such a positive setting. This pivotal moment in our relationship must have also been incredibly difficult for him. I sensed his discomfort and watched from the corner of my eye as he attempted to leave the venue with my mother. In hindsight, he was clearly a man struggling with depression—depression that presented as aggression, irritability, and anger rather than sadness.

As an immigrant male working off his internalized emotional blueprint, originating from a patriarchal culture in which men do not show their vulnerability, any attempt to change must have felt like an insurmountable challenge. While I believe his hardwiring meant that his core personality would remain the same, I had always hoped that he would learn to do things differently for his mental health and relationships. For my mother. For us. Even if I am honest with myself, even if he was open to getting help, at that time, there were no realistic, viable clinical options available to him. Looking back, I believe he did the best he could under the circumstances. He was a depressed man whose symptoms were unrecognized, undiagnosed, and untreated. I see that today as a psychotherapist and believe he needed sympathy, compassion, and understanding more than anything else. Viewing him through this lens, I feel tremendous gratitude for his efforts in doing the best he could with the tools he had in his mental toolbox. I accepted that reality, and it was good enough for me to forgive him and myself for our past mistakes in order to build a healthy relationship with each other in the present and the future.

FORGIVENESS

When most people think of forgiving someone, they think of it as an act of giving something up to another person, akin to an apology, when in fact, it is quite the opposite. So, what is forgiveness?

As I often share with my patients and have experienced myself, forgiveness is something you give *yourself* to free your body and mind of the burdens of housing negative emotions such as pain, anger, and resentment, all of which disturb your mental health and relationships. Holding on to and storing these negative and destructive thoughts and feelings take conscious and sometimes unconscious energy and are oppressive! By forgiving others, at times yourself, you are choosing to liberate your body and mind by releasing these negative emotions. You're unf*cking yourself and your relationships *from the inside out*. This is why I believe we should *all* work on forgiveness. Forgiveness is *powerful* and *empowering*! It is ultimately the gift of emotional freedom you give to yourself and your relationships, some of which you may choose to dissolve even or especially after arriving at forgiveness.

"I forgive you and myself; however, I choose not to be with you" is the expression of your power not only to own your role in mistakes of the past, as interpersonal dynamics are not linear, in addition to theirs, but also to recognize that with this knowledge you choose to move forward in a different direction in the present and future.

Now you know more about forgiveness and the importance of it to your mental health and relationships, how do you unf*ck forgiveness? As in this book, the process of forgiveness starts by becoming aware of your negative emotions, acknowledging them, and learning to express them constructively without apologizing for feeling what you feel about the situation. Like most things, I believe to work things out, we need to talk them out, including forgiving others and ourselves. Sometimes this talking out is with professionals, as I needed to do with Dr. Frank, other times it's with friends, family, and of course, the person we choose to forgive. You can forgive yourself and others; the choice is yours. And be patient; forgiving yourself and others takes time, as illustrated by my years of physical and emotional cutoffs with my father.

Although we ultimately chose to forgive each other, it didn't happen overnight and took years of work on both our parts. We *both* had our perspectives, which involved many negative emotions of pain and hurt, *both* being operative words. And yes, of course, I felt I had more to forgive than he did since he was the parent (although, at times, he didn't act much like it). However, I am guessing that he might have had similar feelings; he may have thought that *he* had the most to forgive since I had "failed" him as an "Indian daughter."

I am certain we both had our *mental yardsticks* at play, as most do, before arriving at forgiveness. However, when it was finally time, and I had gone through therapy with Dr. Frank, we were both ready to throw away our mental yardsticks and focus on building a healthy relationship. We arrived at a place of awareness that allowed us to focus on the present and the future—not the past. I did not condone his past choices, but I chose to forgive him and myself, as did he. From that point on, we moved toward *acceptance*, accepting each other for who that person was and not who we wanted the other to be. This leads to the next prescription of unf*cking yourself and relationships to build healthy relationships.

ACCEPTANCE

We can't choose to forgive ourselves and others without *acceptance*. I forgave my father as he forgave me, and we both learned to accept each other for our true selves without an underlying desire and goal to change the other. Acceptance is an interesting concept and has a valid place in a profession that is predicated on helping people create change. I assert that learning to *accept* is a change that is also needed and is of equal importance in our personal and relational growth and development. How so? Aren't they two opposing paths? Not necessarily; the two can work in tandem. I had to "change" how I thought about my father to "accept" him for who he is and vice versa. To arrive at a place of acceptance, both of us had to be more mindful, thoughtful, and respectful of the other's sense of self so that we could enjoy a newfound relationship. Ultimately, I have learned that a core part of working from the inside out is acceptance. Learning to accept parts of ourselves and those we love is as important as creating change in ourselves and our relationships. Acceptance and change are the flip sides of the same coin. I work with individuals, couples, and families to create change in their unhealthy patterns of behavior, in parallel and concert. I often find myself saying to couples:

"The core of your partner is not going to change; however, they can learn to do some things differently, as can you, if you love each other and want to remain in this relationship successfully. Let's identify the things both of you need to accept about the other and work on a plan of acceptance. Once we have done that, we can move forward and focus on the things both of you are willing to do differently to enhance relational fulfillment and decrease conflict."

This goal is best accomplished through effective, face-to-face, verbal conversations in which effective talking and active listening are practiced, true thoughts and feelings have been expressed and listened to, and conflict has been resolved to mutual satisfaction.

If you're feeling confused or conflicted about identifying what needs to be accepted and what needs to be changed mutually, ask yourself if what you're struggling to reconcile is a deal breaker. Deal breakers are major issues and topics such as having children, relocating to a different country, lifestyle choices, and so forth.

This is a familiar clinical dialogue I have been privy to over the past twenty-five-plus years. Personally, I learned a great deal about acceptance and change through my relationship challenges with my father with the guidance of Dr. Frank. With a great deal of effort and focus, I chose to accept my father's core personality and appreciate the changes he did make over time (and that I made) for the sake of our relationship. And, yes, it was difficult as the two opposing forces can create much internal conflict. However, I always knew my desire to have him in my life was greater than my desire to end our relationship. Once I accepted this about myself, I was able to accept my father and our relationship for what it was. Acceptance and change are not mutually exclusive. They can and do coexist.

CONTENTMENT

Working off the premise that as humans, we seek to maximize pleasure and minimize pain, it is no surprise that we find ourselves in constant pursuit of the emotion called *happiness*. Whether it's through the purchase of a house or a pair of shoes, having a specific job or a new relationship, the end goal is the same: we are all searching for something that will make us feel "happy," giving us a sense of euphoria. In my experience, however, I believe happiness is subjective, relative, and can be rather short-lived.

As a therapist, I regularly encounter people who are pursuing this elusive happiness that we often speak of, hear of, and read of in the plethora of books highlighting its importance, our need for it, and how to find it. My patients reasonably assume that I, as a psychotherapist, possess the key to helping them find happiness. "We are not happy," "We want to be happy," and, "Please, help us find happiness" are all sentiments often expressed in my office. To their initial disappointment and ultimate enlightenment, they quickly learn I don't hold the key to this coveted and desired state of being. However, I do hold the key they are searching for to help them unlock their internal power and guide them toward a more attainable and sustainable pursuit—the pursuit of *contentment*.

I believe we need to shift our focus from the "pursuit of happiness" to the "pursuit of contentment." Contentment, according to Wikipedia, is "an emotional state of satisfaction, drawn from being at ease with one's body and mind." Happiness, on the other hand, is the feeling of pure joy. Although they have similar characteristics, they are different. I believe happiness to be fleeting and in a constant state of fluctuation depending on the day's events: one minute happy, the next minute not so much. Contentment, however, in my paradigm, is more stable. It represents an overall sense of satisfaction and fulfillment with one's life despite circumstances and situations that at times leave us feeling unhappy.

It has been my clinical experience that people who live under the umbrella of contentment, accepting happiness as a fluctuating variable, embody an overall sense of positivism about themselves and others. On the contrary, people who are in the pursuit of happiness, when they experience unhappiness, present their whole life as catastrophic when one aspect of their life is experiencing difficulties. I acknowledge that it's not always so simple. There are complicated psychological layers to the ways people process thoughts and feelings, which determine their mindset. However, on a certain level, I believe this awareness is a helpful place to begin. As I say to my patients: "Let's swap this word *happiness* for *contentment*."

As I share with you, I further explain to them that I believe the pursuit of happiness has left many people feeling a sense of disappointment and instability. When the feeling of happiness evaporates, they urgently seek to get it back by replacing the person or thing that they (mis)perceived as causing their unhappiness. As a psychotherapist, I often listen to tales of people's lives who, in their quest for happiness, end their relationships or quit their jobs, only to learn later that they weren't discontent but were experiencing a moment of unhappiness. To avoid such fumbles, ask yourself: "Am I content in my life, overall?" and, "How does happiness fit into my overall feeling of contentment?"

In addition to the pursuit of happiness leading to more unhappiness, this misguided quest has also made people feel and think of others as easily disposable. Why? Because all relationships include not only moments of happiness but also times of unhappiness, the very feeling that they are trying to avoid. If your partner is supposed to make you happy but does not, you might question their value and place in your life. From my clinical experience, this approach does not work and, in fact, creates the opposite of the intended pursuit.

That is why I encourage you to abandon the pursuit of happiness and instead embark on the quest for contentment. Some might say that this sounds like a game of semantics. Happy, content—what's the difference? There is a *big* difference, and learning to focus on contentment can help you change how you think about life and love. Contentment is the umbrella I believe we should all strive to live under. If we do so, we can find security and comfort in knowing that our lives will not be blown away by a fleeting unhappy moment or episode.

For example, overall, I feel very content in my life with my husband, children, and career. However, sometimes I am not happy with their and my choices or actions but am able to recognize that these episodes will not affect my overall feelings of contentment in the relationship. As I accept that there will be moments of happiness and unhappiness, these fleeting moments will not blow over my umbrella of contentment.

With that in mind, allow me to transition to my personal story one more time to contextualize the meaning of these observations regarding some startling self-discoveries I made in a therapy session with Dr. Frank. It's not what you might expect because it didn't happen in the distant past but rather during the writing of this book.

IN SESSION WITH DR. FRANK

After having hugged, as it had been years since I had seen him, we sat in our respective places and resumed as if we had never left off. Now that I was a licensed, seasoned clinician and not a mere student, I felt like more of an equal to Dr. Frank, although I knew I wasn't; he had so many more years of experience over me. It was a false narrative I tried to sell to myself to level the playing field. He was always going to be my therapist and I his patient, and that power differential would last a lifetime. And so it should.

I opened the session.

"Well, it's great to see you, Dr. Frank. I can't believe it's been so many years. So much has happened. I don't know where to start or what to share. I have missed you and our sessions, but I think I am doing well. I think you will be proud of me."

"Anita, it's wonderful to see you, and you know I am proud of you. I expressed that during our last phone call."

"You did, Dr. Frank. Thank you so much. I guess I just needed to hear you say it again. You know me, always looking for validation from the father figures in my life. But I guess some things don't change," I said with a tear in my eye. Silence took over the room as both he and I observed each other as we had done many times in the past. And after a few minutes, he broke the silence.

"You have my validation, and you're right; some things don't change. They are so ingrained in us that they become part of our DNA. And that's OK. We need to work on accepting them, embracing them, acknowledging them, and living with them in a manner that is not destructive to our lives."

"Wow, you haven't changed a bit, Dr. Frank—not that you needed to. You went right into it, no beating around the bush. I have always loved that about you. I am like that, too, in my practice. My confrontational style works for some and not for others. Being here with you after all these years brings back so many memories." I got him up to speed on my life and shared many stories, eventually bringing the session back to my father, a relationship he helped me to navigate for years. "Getting back to validation and acceptance, Dr. Frank, I am glad that my father and I, to a large degree, have forgiven and accepted each other for who we are. It doesn't mean we are happy with each other all the time, only that we are content overall with our relationship. Isn't that what we should all strive to be—content and not happy?"

"I agree that the pursuit of happiness is self-defeating and leads to more unhappiness. And I am glad to hear that you and your father were in a good place before his passing. That makes the grieving process easier."

"Me too. Otherwise, I would be . . . I don't even want to go there. So what do you think about this whole happiness thing? It's what I encourage all my patients to do: pivot from pursuing happiness to pursuing contentment. Do you love it?"

"What do you think of it?"

"I love it, of course, because I believe in it."

"Then you don't need my approval, although it's clear you're still seeking it."

"OK, then why not just give it to me, Dr. Frank?" I asked with a smile. "Seriously, I accept that I will always be in search of approval from father figures. Maybe you need to accept that about me. I accept it about myself. I know I have to keep it in check and tuck all that shit in when needed, but here with you, it's fair game. I can and should get untucked. Yes?"

"I do, and you're right, Anita," he said, reflecting my smile with his.

It warmed my heart to hear those words from him. After a few more back-and-forths, the session ended, and it was time to say goodbye. We hugged, and I looked around his office one last time and realized nothing other than me had changed. I was no longer that fearful little girl but a strong woman who had reconciled her past with the present. I had come a long way since our first session. Although I still sought his approval, I did not need it to live my life. I had done perfectly fine without him all these years. But had I been without him? Not really! His voice, the office, and our work together remain etched in my psyche and serve as the new "blueprint" for my internal and external psychological workings. Our therapeutic relationship taught me the true meaning of building healthy relationships from the inside out, although I did not have the words to describe it then as I do now. I've reflected on our sessions throughout the years, there is no doubt in my mind that it's not a coincidence that I became a professional therapist.

My father's behavior and my family dynamics consciously and unconsciously sparked my deep curiosity about human nature. He was a complex man who was highly conflicted. His plight impacted me to such a great degree that it drove my burning desire to do something worthy with my life. And I believe I have, even as I strive to be more and do more. I have finally come to realize, accept, and be content knowing that I am my father's daughter.

* * *

CHAPTER 7 WORKSHEET: FORGIVENESS, ACCEPTANCE, AND CONTENTMENT

1. What does forgiveness mean for you?

2. Have you forgiven yourself for past mistakes?

3. Is there anyone that you need to forgive in your life?

4. If yes, what's holding you back?

5. Do you believe that acceptance and change can coexist? Please explain.

6. Did you feel accepted in your family of origin? If not, how come?

7. Do you feel accepted by them now? If not, how come?

8. What does acceptance mean to you today?

9. Have you accepted yourself, the good, the bad, and the ugly (we all have these parts)?

10. If not, which parts of yourself are you most uncomfortable accepting?

11. Do you feel accepted in your current relationship(s)? If not, how come?

12. Have you practiced accepting others for who they are?

13. Are you *stuck* in the cycle of the *pursuit of happiness*?

14. What does contentment mean to you?

15. Are you content in and with your life?

CONGRATULATIONS!

You're on your way to unf*cking your
life and relationships from the inside
out and getting back to the basics
of life and love by incorporating the
seven prescriptions shared with you in
this book. Let your journey of change
continue successfully outside these
pages with commitment, determination,
desire, passion, consistency,
compassion, and strength.

SUMMARY

THIS BOOK is the culmination of over twenty-five years of clinical experience with couples, individuals, and families and my life's journey of unf*cking myself and my relationships through individual psychotherapy. From my hands to your hands, from my life to your life, I have shared my story of adversity and resilience with the goal of empowering and inspiring you to build healthy relationships from the inside out, *not* from the outside in! Reversal of this order, in my professional and personal experience, only serves history repeating itself through recreating and replaying similar and familiar dynamics both consciously and unconsciously. My individual therapeutic experience with Dr. Frank helped to minimize my risk of repeating dysfunctional patterns of thinking, feeling, and behaving; accepting unhealthy relationships as healthy; settling for faulty communication styles; and internalizing an unrealistic perception of myself and others. Through my work with him I was able to heal my "wounded inner child" and live my adult life free, as much as one can be, from the voices of my past that served to do more emotional and relational harm than good. Those negative

SUMMARY

voices were replaced by one powerful voice: mine and mine alone, one that I had been afraid to own, acknowledge, and use to take control of my life and my relationships. Although I have occasional mental slips here and there when I'm triggered, I am *mostly* unf*cked and enjoy healthy relationships.

Unf*cking myself and my relationships, however, did not happen overnight, nor was it a painless process, as I share with my patients when they ask me questions such as: "How long will this take?" and, "How come, at times, I feel worse after seeing you?"

I understand these concerns all too well from an experiential and academic stance as my individual therapy was taking place in parallel to my clinical training. I was literally on both sides of the couch; a unique experience to say the least. Anyway, I, too, had similar questions and conflicted feelings about therapy which Dr. Frank helped me to untangle early on. I questioned its efficacy, my commitment, and, most importantly, my ability and willingness to tolerate being emotionally and psychologically challenged by a father figure such as a clinician, given my conflicted relationship with my dad. Dr. Frank confronted all that I was trying to repress, hide, run away from, and was familiar with. I very quickly learned that similarity and familiarity breed comfort even in circumstances that make us uncomfortable and the need for things to change rapidly and the desire to avoid pain whenever possible are natural predispositions. These predispositions are in constant challenge in a process that takes time. In addition to time, I discovered that *change* commands commitment, determination, dedication, strength, and the ability and willingness to confront rather than avoid our reflection in the mirror. Fortunately, I had just enough self-awareness to acknowledge that I needed to resolve my issues not only for my mental health and relationships but for the benefit of my future patients.

I also knew that I did not want to live my adult life like I had lived my childhood. So, yes, it did get worse at times during my therapeutic process before it got better. How can it not when you're forced to confront that which you spent most of your life running from? However, I assure you that it *does* get better as it will for you once you begin your unf*cking process. I am living proof and my personal and professional experiences serve as testimony.

Break the cycle or perpetuate it. The choice is yours. Change comes with the unknown, and the unknown is often fraught with fear. I know this well. I lived most of my younger years in this space. Challenge yourself, as I later did, to choose the unknown; confront that which you fear. You might surprise yourself as your resourcefulness and resilience emerge. You're stronger than you think! You're better and more than your past has led you to believe within yourself and with others.

As you have surmised by now through reading this book, building healthy relationships with others means you have to embrace and work through all parts of yourself—the good, the bad, the ugly, the complicated, the conflicted, and whatever else you may be feeling and projecting on to others. An integrated self is a "whole self," and a whole self is better equipped and able to join with others in healthy relationships. I believe that our

SUMMARY

mental health hinges on the quality of our relationships. They are linked—the flip sides of the same coin resulting in a unique interpersonal dance you invite others to join. At times the footwork is in sync; other times it is not. This interpersonal dance is a reflection of your past clashing with your present; your inner child at war with your adult self who is emotionally paralyzed to take different actions. Making a different choice requires you to engage in introspection for the purpose of reaching a level of awareness that serves to unf*ck your mind by owning your shit and your projections and rejecting other peoples' projections onto you. This requires you to get comfortable with negative thoughts and feelings that you most likely were taught to repress; hence, your projections. Dr. Frank helped me to unf*ck my old ways of thinking and feeling about negativity and aggression and encouraged me to accept parts of myself that I had rejected. I encourage you to do the same: acknowledge your negative thoughts and feelings, accept them for what they are and their origins, and keep them in check. By doing so, you will not allow them to negatively govern nor define your interactions with others and will reduce passive-aggressive behaviors on your part in the present. It's OK! We are all by nature aggressive. Our ability to take responsibility, manage, and express aggression will determine the impact and outcome it has on our relationships. Do it without the use of verbal disguises and in a constructive (not destructive) manner as outlined in this book.

Once you can accomplish this, you will quickly be able to recognize that which does not belong to you emotionally. You'll soon learn to reject other peoples' projections on to you by not

SUMMARY

only establishing your emotional and physical boundaries but keeping them in check as some people in your life may seek to violate them. Why? Because as you change from the inside out, you will radiate a more confident, strong, resilient *self*, which some people might take issue with as they try to bring you back to the person you used to be, in essence sabotaging your success because it makes them uncomfortable.

"That's a 'you problem,' not mine!"

This is a statement I encourage you to use, as I do my patients, during the process of change when experiencing a violation of boundaries via projections and passive-aggressive behaviors. As you have learned, physical and emotional boundaries are necessary and serve to protect us and our relationships from physical and emotional harm. Boundaries help reduce conflict by identifying rules of engagement—what is allowed and what is not—and how that information is managed and talked about. When boundaries are not clear or established or there is a boundary violation, conflict naturally arises.

The next step within yourself and in your relationships is to seek resolution, which is challenging for most as it requires us, I believe, to talk to each other. Unfortunately, the current trend, based on the stories brought to me by my patients and my observations and experiences, is that people seek to resolve conflict without uttering words, only exchanging them in written form via texts and other forms of e-communications. Although the value of electronic communication is undeniable, as proven during the pandemic, it cannot and should not be used to replace the simple act of talking. Attempts at

SUMMARY

doing so do *not* work and often create further complications and additional miscommunications. My clinical experiences over the past twenty-five-plus years guide my belief that this is best accomplished through effective, face-to-face, verbal conversations in which effective talking and active listening are practiced. Doing so leaves each person feeling that their true thoughts and feelings have been expressed and listened to, which will make arriving at mutual satisfactory resolutions less complicated. Let's work toward making verbal conversation the norm again and use electronic communication with specific boundaries. I believe both can and should coexist to enhance our relationships without compromising them.

As you follow each of my prescriptions, you will realize the connection and interplay of one to the other as each serve as building blocks. Once you're able to effectively verbally communicate with others, you can work toward having a more open and honest conversation about identifying and sharing your needs and expectations. Knowing one another's needs and expectations is vital to building, maintaining, nurturing, and sustaining healthy relationships. I am often surprised in session when couples are clueless about their partner's needs and expectations. It's been my experience that this is usually a function of how their needs and expectations were handled in their family of origin, as shared previously. If, as a child, your needs and expectations were never taken into consideration, then you will carry this belief about them into your adult relationships. I often say:

"As a child you had no choice but to repress your needs

and expectations but as an adult you do. Give yourself permission to have them, then identify them and share them with your significant others."

And, yes, your needs and expectations will be different from your partner's in certain areas. As long as they are not foundational differences, it's OK! No two people are the same. It's accepting these differences, rather than trying to change them, that helps the relationship to be successful. Accepting the other for who they are at their core within the framework of change is part of maintaining and nurturing healthy relationships and being content . . . not happy. I believe happiness in relationships and life in general is an unrealistic and defeating pursuit. Our search and pursuit of it, in my opinion and experience, only lead to more unhappiness. Hence, I propose we pursue an overall state of contentment and abandon the notion of being the "happy couple and person" to being a "content couple and person." I believe it's a more realistic state of being and one which can be achieved with success.

In conclusion, I am confident that my words will inspire and motivate you to get back to the basics of life and love for your mental health and your desire to build, nurture, and maintain healthy relationships. By committing to stay on that path as you follow my prescriptions, you will discover your authentic self, a self that can join in harmony with others as a lover, friend, sibling, adult child, coworker, and more. Relationships are all around us, and you are in and around them. They are not exclusive to romance. As such, it's of grave importance that you learn to navigate them to live a balanced,

SUMMARY

healthy life and accept that change is a continuous process. Accept this reality and begin by:

Step 1. Becoming self-aware through introspection.

Step 2. Owning your projections, rejecting other people's projections onto you, and working through your passive-aggressive expressions and actions.

Step 3. Improving verbal communication through active listening and effective talking.

Step 4. Identifying, establishing, and discussing needs and expectations.

Step 5. Identifying, establishing, enforcing, and maintaining healthy boundaries.

Step 6. Embracing, confronting, and resolving conflict rather than avoiding it.

Step 7. Forgiving yourself and others, accepting core parts of the self/others, and pursuing contentment instead of happiness.

As you follow these seven prescriptions, remember that you are the writer of your narrative and how you bring that script to life is your choice, a choice that will impact your relationships. Write your narrative and then rewrite it as you unf*ck yourself and relationships from the inside out. *You* are the book. Turn the page.

ACKNOWLEDGMENTS

I WOULD LIKE to begin by thanking each patient who has thus far entrusted me with their life stories, along with their hopes and aspirations for a better and brighter future. In essence, this book is a result of our work together. I feel privileged to have worked with each and every one of you.

Next, I would like to recognize the invaluable assistance of Larry Morton, CEO of Hal Leonard. Larry's years of experience in the publishing world helped propel this project from a manuscript on my desk to this book that you're reading today. I am eternally grateful to you for your expert guidance, insightful feedback, time, belief in me and goals, and ultimately serving as the person who would bring the Ask Anita Astley (A3) team together, beginning with John Cerullo, my my publishing consultant and editorial guide. I would like to extend my deepest gratitude to John for having faith in my work and for helping navigate my publishing journey by always filling in the blind spots, ensuring that the project stayed on course, offering ongoing encouragement and support, for sharing his valuable time with A3 when it was needed, and most importantly, for

ACKNOWLEDGMENTS

paying very close attention to detail.

I would also like to thank Rey Taylor not only for his editorial work but for the hours of bantering on the phone in an effort to get the work done. I have appreciated your creativity, keen insights, and emotional support. Additional thanks to David Michaels for his initial work on this book.

I would also like to pay special thanks to Peter Giles for his overall support in brand management, editorial assistance, and, most of all, for bringing my dream of the "Orange Chair" campaign to life in Times Square. I couldn't have done it without you!

Also, my thanks to Forefront Books and the Simon & Schuster team, which helped bring my book to market. Special thanks to Jennifer Gingerich, the editorial director at Forefront Books, for her patience and understanding during the editorial process process. Also, many thanks to the team at Smith Publicity for their dedication, commitment, and hard work in promoting my book.

These acknowledgments would not be complete without extending my deepest gratitude to Dr. Mark Aulls. You helped me to believe in myself and my abilities to succeed academically and in life when I didn't believe in myself. The countless hours you invested in me during our summer research project went above and beyond the call of duty. You played a pivotal role helping me become the person I am today. I feel blessed to have you as my mentor.

I am also extremely grateful to my dear friend and colleague of many years Dr. David Steindorf. Thank you for

ACKNOWLEDGMENTS

reviewing my manuscript in its early stages, for your detailed and insightful feedback, your words of support and encouragement, and most of all, your time.

To my family, thank you for always believing in my dreams and always loving me: Ashwani, Poonam, Sunil. And a special thank you to Diana Lyrintzis, my sister-in-law, for sharing her legal mind with me in the early stages of this journey.

Special thanks to all of my friends, who are like family, for their interest, support, patience, and, most important, for listening to me when I just needed to talk about the challenges of work and life.

My thanks to Cody Sexton, Tim Weber, John Seltenreich, and Alia Rouf for their editorial reviews, and much gratitude to Tia Lee for her amazing cover photo shoot. Thanks as well to my legal advisor, Ellis Levine, for his guidance on this project.

The final three people I would like to recognize are my children, William and Sarah, and my husband, Oliver.

William, I am grateful for that conversation we had that day in the kitchen in which you told me to take my advice. I did! And look what's happened! You are your mother's son.

Sarah, I am beyond grateful for your patience, understanding, independence, and ability to get things done when I was knee-deep in my writing. You're an inspiration and an incredible young woman.

And finally, I would like to express my deepest gratitude to my husband, Oliver Astley, for his love, unwavering support, patience, words of encouragement, and belief in my dreams.

ENDNOTES

1. Robbins, Tom. Cited online at https://www.goodreads.com/quotes/12019-when-we-re-incomplete-we-re-always-searching-for-somebody-to-complete.

2. Jung, Carl. *Modern Man in Search of a Soul* (1933). Accessed online June 27, 2022, in *Oxford Essential Quotations* (Oxford University Press, 2016). https://www.oxfordreference.com/view/10.1093/acref/9780191826719.001.0001/q-oro-ed4-00006107

3. Robbins, Tony. Twitter post, February 13, 2018, https://twitter.com/tonyrobbins/status/963428301321768961.

4. Frankl, Viktor. *Man's Search for Meaning* (Boston: Beacon Press, 1962).